✧ *Companions for the Journey* ✧

Praying with
Catherine McAuley

✧ *Companions for the Journey* ✧

Praying with Catherine McAuley

by
Helen Marie Burns, RSM
and
Sheila Carney, RSM

Saint Mary's Press
Christian Brothers Publications
Winona, Minnesota

✦ *To our mothers* ✦
Helen Margaret Ryan Burns
and
Margaret Mawe Carney,
First Teachers of Mercy

The publishing team for this book included Carl Koch, development editor; Rosemary Wallner, copy editor; Amy Schlumpf Manion, production editor and typesetter; Maurine Twait, art director; Elaine Kohner, illustrator; pre-press, printing, and binding by the graphics division of Saint Mary's Press.

The scriptural material found on pages 38, 53, 58–59, 106, and 118 is freely adapted and is not to be understood or used as an official translation of the Bible.

All other scriptural quotations used in this book are from the New Jerusalem Bible. Copyright © 1985 by Darton, Longman & Todd, London; and Doubleday, a division of Bantam, Doubleday, Dell Publishing Group, New York. Used with permission.

The acknowledgments continue on page 121.

Printed in the United States of America

Printing: 9 8 7 6 5 4 3 2 1

Year: 2004 03 02 01 00 99 98 97 96

ISBN 0-88489-334-0

✧ Contents ✧

✧ Foreword ✧

Companions for the Journey

Just as food is required for human life, so are companions. Indeed, the word *companions* comes from two Latin words: *com*, meaning "with," and *panis*, meaning "bread." Companions nourish our heart, mind, soul, and body. They are also the people with whom we can celebrate the sharing of bread.

Perhaps the most touching stories in the Bible are about companionship: the Last Supper, the wedding feast at Cana, the sharing of the loaves and the fishes, and Jesus' breaking of bread with the disciples on the road to Emmaus. Each incident of companionship with Jesus revealed more about his mercy, love, wisdom, suffering, and hope. When Jesus went to pray in the Garden of Olives, he craved the companionship of the Apostles. They let him down. But God sent the Spirit to inflame the hearts of the Apostles, and they became faithful companions to Jesus and to each other.

Throughout history, other faithful companions have followed Jesus and the Apostles. These saints and mystics have also taken the journey from conversion, through suffering, to resurrection. Just as they were inspired by the holy people who went before them, so too may you take them as your companions as you walk on your spiritual journey.

The Companions for the Journey series is a response to the spiritual hunger of Christians. This series makes available the rich spiritual teachings of mystics and guides whose wisdom can help us on our pilgrimages. As you complete the last meditation in each volume, it is hoped that you will feel supported, challenged, and affirmed by a soul-companion on your spiritual journey.

The spiritual hunger that has emerged over the last twenty years is a great sign of renewal in Christian life. People fill retreat programs and workshops on topics in spirituality. The demand for spiritual directors exceeds the number available. Interest in the lives and writings of saints and mystics is increasing as people search for models of whole and holy Christian life.

Praying with Catherine McAuley

Praying with Catherine McAuley is more than just a book about Catherine's spirituality. This book seeks to engage you in praying in the way that Catherine did about issues and themes that were central to her experience. Each meditation can enlighten your understanding of her spirituality and lead you to reflect on your own experience.

The goal of *Praying with Catherine McAuley* is that you will discover Catherine's rich spirituality and integrate her spirit and wisdom into your relationship with God, with your brothers and sisters, and with your own heart and mind.

Suggestions for Praying with Catherine

Meet Catherine McAuley, a fascinating companion for your pilgrimage, by reading the introduction to this book, which begins on page 14. It provides a brief biography of Catherine and an outline of the major themes of her spirituality.

Once you meet Catherine, you will be ready to pray with her and to encounter God, your sisters and brothers, and yourself in new and wonderful ways. To help your prayer, here are some suggestions that have been part of the tradition of Christian spirituality:

Create a sacred space. Jesus said, "'When you pray, go to your private room, shut yourself in, and so pray to your [God] who is in that secret place, and your [God] who sees all that is done in secret will reward you'" (Matthew 6:6). Solitary prayer is best done in a place where you can have privacy and silence, both of which can be luxuries in the life of busy people. If privacy and silence are not possible, create a quiet, safe place within yourself, perhaps while riding to and from work, while sitting in line at the dentist's office, or while waiting for someone. Do the best you can, knowing that a loving God is present everywhere. Whether the meditations in this book are used for solitary prayer or with a group, try to create a prayerful mood with candles, meditative music, an open Bible, or a crucifix.

Open yourself to the power of prayer. Every human experience has a religious dimension. All of life is suffused with God's presence. So remind yourself that God is present as you begin your period of prayer. Do not worry about distractions. If something keeps intruding during your prayer, spend some time talking with God about it. Be flexible because God's Spirit blows where it will.

Prayer can open your mind and widen your vision. Be open to new ways of seeing God, people, and yourself. As you open yourself to the Spirit of God, different emotions are evoked, such as sadness from tender memories, or joy from a celebration recalled. Our emotions are messages from God that can tell us much about our spiritual quest. Also, prayer strengthens our will to act. Through prayer, God can touch our will and empower us to live according to what we know is true.

Finally, many of the meditations in this book will call you to employ your memories, your imagination, and the circumstances of your life as subjects for prayer. The great mystics and saints realized that they had to use all their resources to know God better. Indeed, God speaks to us continually and touches us constantly. We must learn to listen and feel with all the means that God has given us.

Come to prayer with an open mind, heart, and will.

Preview each meditation before beginning. After you have placed yourself in God's presence, spend a few moments previewing the readings and especially the reflection activities. Several reflection activities are given in each meditation because different styles of prayer appeal to different personalities or personal needs. **Note that each meditation has more reflection activities than can be done during one prayer**

period. Therefore, select only one or two reflection activities each time you use a meditation. **Do not feel compelled to complete all the reflection activities**.

Read meditatively. Each meditation offers you a story about Catherine and a reading from her writings. Take your time reading. If a particular phrase touches you, stay with it. Relish its feelings, meanings, and concerns.

Use the reflections. Following the readings is a short reflection in commentary form, which is meant to give perspective to the readings. Then you are offered several ways of meditating on the readings and the theme of the prayer. You may be familiar with the different methods of meditating, but in case you are not, they are described briefly here:

✦ *Repeated short prayer or mantra:* One means of focusing your prayer is to use a *mantra,* or "prayer word." The mantra may be a single word or a short phrase taken from the readings or from the Scriptures. For example, a short prayer for meditation 3 in this book is "Faithful Provider." Repeated slowly in harmony with your breathing, the mantra helps you center your heart and mind on one action or attribute of God.

✦ *Lectio divina:* This type of meditation is "divine studying," a concentrated reflection on the word of God or the wisdom of a spiritual writer. Most often in *lectio divina,* you will be invited to read one of the passages several times and then concentrate on one or two sentences, pondering their meaning for you and their effect on you. *Lectio divina* commonly ends with formulation of a resolution.

✦ *Guided meditation:* In this type of meditation, our imagination helps us consider alternative actions and likely consequences. Our imagination helps us experience new ways of seeing God, our neighbors, ourselves, and nature. When Jesus told his followers parables and stories, he engaged their imagination. In this book, you will be invited to follow guided meditations.

One way of doing a guided meditation is to read the scene or story several times, until you know the outline and can recall it when you enter into reflection. Or before your prayer time, you may wish to record the meditation on a tape recorder. If so, remember to allow pauses for reflection between phrases and to speak with a slow, peaceful pace and tone. Then, during prayer, when you have finished the readings and the reflection commentary, you can turn on your recording of the meditation and be led through it. If you find your own voice too distracting, ask a friend to make the tape for you.

✦ *Examen of consciousness:* The reflections often will ask you to examine how God has been speaking to you in your past and present experience—in other words, the reflections will ask you to examine your awareness of God's presence in your life.

✦ *Journal writing:* Writing is a process of discovery. If you write for any length of time, stating honestly what is on your mind and in your heart, you will unearth much about who you are, how you stand with your God, what deep longings reside in your soul, and more. In some reflections, you will be asked to write a dialog with Jesus or someone else. If you have never used writing as a means of meditation, try it. Reserve a special notebook for your journal writing. If desired, you can go back to your entries at a future time for an examen of consciousness.

✦ *Action:* Occasionally, a reflection will suggest singing a favorite hymn, going out for a walk, or undertaking some other physical activity. Actions can be meaningful forms of prayer.

Using the Meditations for Group Prayer

If you wish to use the meditations for community prayer, these suggestions may help:

✦ Read the theme to the group. Call the community into the presence of God, using the short opening prayer. Invite one or two participants to read one or both readings. If you use both readings, observe the pause between them.

✦ The reflection commentary may be used as a reading, or it can be deleted, depending on the needs and interests of the group.

✦ Select one of the reflection activities for your group. Allow sufficient time for your group to reflect, to recite a centering prayer or mantra, to accomplish a studying prayer *(lectio divina)*, or to finish an examen of consciousness. Depending on the group and the amount of available time, you may want to invite the participants to share their reflections, responses, or petitions with the group.

✦ Reading the passage from the Scriptures may serve as a summary of the meditation.

✦ The closing prayer may be recited by the entire group. Or you may ask participants to offer their own prayers for the closing.

Now you are ready to begin praying with Catherine McAuley, a faithful and caring companion on this stage of your spiritual journey. It is hoped that you will find her to be a true soul-companion.

CARL KOCH
Editor

✧ Preface ✧

When Catherine McAuley founded the Sisters of Mercy, she instilled within the community the very difficult dynamic of an equal emphasis on action and contemplation. This creative tension was rooted in the life of Jesus with its alternation of prayerful withdrawal and loving presence. This rhythm must beat in our hearts if we would follow Jesus and Catherine.

The meditations comprising this book call us into this rhythm, offering material for reflection and prayer, then challenging us to put the insights and graces received into practice. We invite you to enter into them with energy and imagination, knowing that they can lead you on the path of mercy.

For the life of mercy that has been planted and nurtured in us, we are grateful to the members of the Institute of the Sisters of Mercy of the Americas, particularly the women of the Regional Communities of Detroit and Pittsburgh.

And a thousand thanks to Pat Jones who, with warm encouragement, reviving humor, and invaluable technical assistance, was our good companion in this project.

✧ Introduction ✧

Catherine Elizabeth McAuley is a woman for our era as well as her own. The Ireland of her day foreshadowed many elements of a twentieth-century socioeconomic reality. A contemporary journalist might have seen the headlines possible in the events of Catherine's life: "Heiress Turns Fortune to Folly," "Callaghan Family Challenges Caretaker's Claim to Estate," "Prominent Surgeon Threatens House Guest," "Dublin Socialite Evades Solicitors," and "Baggot Street Ladies Criticized by Local Clergy."

However, in her own time, Catherine's story was more quietly noted and appreciated. Catherine McAuley is remarkable for the manner in which she embodied the ordinary virtues in her daily life. What was said of her shortly after her death could be said of many faithful women and men: "She was convinced that Almighty God required her to make some lasting efforts for the relief of the suffering and instruction of the ignorant" (Angela Bolster, *Catherine McAuley in Her Own Words*, p. 31). She felt called, in other words, to make some contribution to the well-being of the world in which she found herself.

The beauty of her story and her person grew, according to an early biographer, as flowers in a garden, gradually and almost imperceptibly:

> The ten short years of her own religious life were but the seeding-time; it was only after her death that the full fruitfulness of her life began to show itself. At the time of her death there were little more than 100 Sisters of Mercy; fifteen years later there were 3,000 . . . one hundred years later there were 23,000. (Roland Burke Savage, *Catherine McAuley: The First Sister of Mercy*, p. 393)

14

This garden metaphor reflects Catherine's own love for growth and beauty. Her letters and writings contain many passages in which the spiritual life is described in garden images and the dedicated soul as "an enclosed garden where all the virtues flourish" (Angela Bolster, *Positio*, vol. 1, p. 841). Garden imagery, then, seems a fitting metaphor by which to unfold the story of her life.

Preparing the Soil

Rich Celtic soil nurtured the flower of Catherine McAuley's spirit and personality. Her family traced their lineage from ancient princes, warriors, and nobility. Catherine, born on 29 September 1778, matured in the early decades of the nineteenth century. Unemployment was high in Ireland, especially in urban areas where poorhouses and workhouses multiplied as fast as factories. Rapid industrialization as well as crop failure impelled hundreds of farmers to migrate toward urban areas for assistance and employment. Social and religious prejudice was pervasive, fueled by years of legalized discrimination. Uneven educational opportunities, neighborhood decay, and urban and rural tensions resulted from both discrimination and migration.

Extreme wealth and extreme poverty marked the social and economic reality of Ireland, straining the few welfare systems available. Modern progress eased life's burdens for some, while civil war, political unrest, and disease weakened the support systems of many others, mainly women and children. Persons of means often viewed poor people with condescension and distaste. Unrest and suffering abounded in the streets and homes of the disadvantaged, while the wealthy enjoyed fashionable food, clothing, and entertainment.

In the decades before Catherine's birth, the repeal of the British Penal Laws had begun. Freed from these laws that suppressed Catholicism and promoted the Church of England, the Catholic church once again enjoyed legitimate standing as an institution of faith and service. Its clergy, members, and practices were no longer subject to legal sanctions, nor barred from public expression. However, prejudicial attitudes embedded in societal structures continue to mark the experience of Irish Catholics even today. Catholic Church leaders seized the moment to revitalize and renew Catholic identity, self-esteem, and influence. A significant piece of their plan for revitalizing the faith centered on caring for basic needs of impoverished masses and providing educational opportunities for children. According to Angela Bolster, author of the *Positio* prepared for the canonization of Catherine McAuley:

> This [1820–1830] was a decade of religious revival, spearheaded by Dr. Daniel Murray [Archbishop of Dublin] . . . [whose] remedy for the spiritual malnutrition in his diocese was to revive the sacramental life of the people and to increase the number of clergy, churches and schools in his diocese. (P. 66)

Into this Ireland and this church, Catherine McAuley was born.

Planting the Seeds

Catherine's early years reflected the careful seeding of Catholic upbringing. Her father, James McAuley, was an ardent practitioner of his faith and, it would appear, a shrewd entrepreneur. Catholics, even under the restrictions of the Penal Laws, were allowed to engage in trade and in nonprofessional activities. Within those parameters, James McAuley provided comfortable, upper middle-class circumstances for his wife, Elinor, and their three children, Catherine, Mary, and James.

Catherine cherished memories of her father as a sensitive and generous man who gathered the children of the neighboring slums around the tree in his front yard to teach them the mysteries of their faith. Her mother, thirty years younger than her husband, was lovely, charming, and gracious. She was also somewhat pampered by her husband and family, and quite unprepared for the responsibility of single-parenting that James's death in 1783 thrust upon her.

The death of James McAuley and Elinor's inability to manage her financial matters occasioned a gradual descent into poverty for the McAuley family. Within the year after her husband's death, Elinor McAuley sold the Stormanstown House and moved to a smaller place nearby. Three years later she and the children moved into Dublin to Queen Street to be near Elinor's friend, a Mrs. St. George. Each successive residence was smaller than Stormanstown, but they were new homes in bustling neighborhoods. Catherine and her siblings seem to have adjusted to their new circumstances with the resilience natural to young people. For a few years, life returned to the comfort of routine.

Although Elinor saw to the sacramental education of her children (the Eucharist and confirmation), she neglected the full practice of Catholicism and offered little resistance to the sharp criticism of her faith offered by Anglican and Protestant friends and relatives. Catherine alone seemed to have minded the anti-Catholic attitudes and conversations of their Dublin milieu.

When Elinor McAuley's health failed, her lengthy illness threatened the family's stability. Elinor had to sell the house on Queen Street in 1796. She and her children moved into the home of her brother, Dr. Owen Conway, where Catherine cared for her mother and her siblings. The care of her mother was particularly difficult for young Catherine, as Elinor's remorseful conscience brought much anguish of soul in her last months of life.

By the time of Elinor's death in 1798, the eldest McAuley daughter had become guardian to her siblings, nurse and confidante for her mother, and an eligible young woman in Dublin's social circles. However, the McAuley family hung precariously on the edge of destitution and dispersal. Catherine herself moved into an uncertain future with a twofold legacy:

> Her father's religious fervor crossed with her mother's intellectual independence; her mother's gentility and ability to associate in society crossed with her father's identification and involvement with the poor, the outcast and the downtrodden. (Joanna Regan and Isabelle Keiss, *Tender Courage: A Reflection on the Life and Spirit of Catherine McAuley, First Sister of Mercy,* p. 14)

Germination

The loss of their parents caused the dispersal of the McAuley children. Catherine's sister and brother moved into the home of a distant Protestant relative, William Armstrong. Catherine separated from her siblings in order to remain with the Catholic family of Dr. Owen Conway. This separation left great pain and, for Catherine, opened the way to a spiraling decline in financial circumstances.

Catherine enjoyed the companionship of the Conway's daughter, Anne, with whom she entered the rounds of fashionable parties and social events for teenagers among Dublin's upper class. Suitors and fond acquaintances surrounded the two young women at these many stylish affairs. Later, in her letters to her colleagues in Mercy, Catherine would indicate ample knowledge of the dance steps as well as the musical airs of her time.

Despite this gaiety, tension and suffering permeated the Conway household. Dr. Conway gambled and drank. Before he finally declared bankruptcy, his family often lacked adequate food and experienced the embarrassment of irate creditors and repossession of furnishings. Little more than a year after her arrival at the Conways, Catherine found herself forced to join her sister and brother in the Armstrong home.

At the Armstrongs', well-meaning Anglican relatives sought to convert the McAuley children to their faith and, consequently, the social and economic status associated with it. The financial and social elite of eighteenth-century Dublin were Anglican, and many of them viewed Catholics as generally wallowing in poverty, superstition, and bad taste. The Armstrongs shared these prejudices and wished better for their orphaned relatives.

Catherine, more than her siblings, seems to have resisted such pressure. In the face of steady, often scornful proselytizing, Catherine regretted that her own lack of education prevented her from effectively defending the faith she held with such conviction.

When she was twenty-five, an opportunity presented itself that considerably altered Catherine's spiritual development and material status. William and Catherine Callaghan, acquaintances of the Armstrongs, were attracted to Catherine's vivacity and graciousness. When they decided to move their residence to Coolock House, a country estate, they asked Catherine to join them. Envisioned in their invitation was the expectation that she would be a companion to Mrs. Callaghan, who was chronically ill, and would assume some responsibilities for their household. Catherine saw in this position a means of establishing a degree of independence for herself as well as an opportunity to utilize skills learned in the care of her mother. She most likely did not anticipate the twenty-year commitment to the Callaghan household, nor the mutual love that would lead William Callaghan and his wife to offer their name as well as their wealth to Miss McAuley.

Growing

Life with the Callaghans, who were Protestant, continued the pain of an unfamiliar religious context. However, unlike the Armstrongs, the Callaghans eventually consented to Catherine's practice of the Catholic faith, providing that she brought no signs of popery into their household. Catherine eagerly embraced this restriction in order to practice her faith openly without ridicule. She also sought spiritual counsel from several priests who were instrumental in helping her to articulate her Catholic belief.

In the service of the poor, which began to occupy Catherine's leisure time, she and the Callaghans found no tension or disagreement. She was encouraged in her desire to offer her free time to the poor school in the area and to visit the homes of poor families for whom the Callaghans provided food, clothing, and medicine. The Callaghans also tolerated Catherine's generous outreach to orphaned relatives and her efforts to support the children of her sister, Mary.

When a dear cousin, Anne Conway Byrn, died of tuberculosis, Catherine adopted her four children. The Callaghans allowed Catherine to bring the children to Coolock House and also agreed to the addition of two orphans whom Catherine had befriended from the Coolock village. Catherine seems to have had her father's love for and natural rapport with young people who, as one biographer observes, "revealed their tribulations to her" (Carmel Bourke, *A Woman Sings of Mercy: Reflections on the Life and Spirit of Mother Catherine McAuley, Foundress of the Sisters of Mercy*, p. 4).

Catherine created a network of services for poor people in the neighborhood of Coolock House. She also gathered young girls from the neighborhood, taught them needlework, and then proceeded to open a shop on the Coolock estate to sell their handiwork. Unobtrusively, the seeds planted in Catherine's childhood—seeds of generosity, practical faith, gracious love of poor, sick, and uneducated persons—were germinating toward a full flowering.

During her twenty years as a companion in the Callaghan household, Catherine was exposed to Mrs. Callaghan's Quaker faith and practice. A recent biographer suggests that the Quaker respect and appreciation for the talents of women may have been particularly important in shaping Catherine's sense of service. It seems probable that her awareness that the Quaker "Women's Meetings" were charged with concern for the poor of their own sex may have inspired Catherine's oft-quoted maxim: "Nothing is more productive of good to society than the careful instruction of [poor] women" (Regan and Keiss, *Tender Courage*, p. 16).

In addition to significant learnings from the Quaker tradition of Mrs. Callaghan, Catherine developed her natural skills for organization, financial management, and nursing. Eventually the Callaghans gave Catherine full responsibility for managing the Coolock properties and, as their health gradually deteriorated, she provided more and more practical nursing care for them.

The deaths of Mrs. Callaghan in 1819 and Mr. Callaghan in 1822 left Catherine once more bereft of those she deeply loved. Her consolation in this instance, however, was to have seen each of them baptized into the Catholic faith on their deathbed. Her own steady faith had made a deep impression on her benefactors and each had embraced its mysteries in their final hours.

The inheritance she eventually received from the Callaghan estate, approximately one million dollars by today's standards, enabled her to focus all her resources and energies on a ministry to the poor, previously the occupation of her leisure time.

Flowering and Fruit

With the Callaghan inheritance, Catherine, at the age of forty-four, began this new phase of life by expanding her charitable efforts in the area of Coolock House. Other women with similar interests joined her in these endeavors. Gradually the idea of using the bulk of her inheritance to create a shelter for their educational endeavors as well as their ministries to orphans and homeless women took possession of Catherine. She was determined to build a home on Baggot Street, bordering a fashionable Dublin neighborhood. The home would serve as a shelter and educational center for young women from poorer neighborhoods of the city. She began supervision of the project even as she continued work on the settlement of the Callaghan estate.

Of immediate concern to Catherine was the failing health of her sister, Mary, now married to a well-known Protestant surgeon, William Macauley, and mother of five young children. Between 1822 and 1827, Catherine divided her time between the care of Mary, the sale of the Coolock House, supervision of her Baggot Street project known as "Kitty's folly" to her family, and volunteer work at Saint Mary's School for Poor Children on Liffey Street.

In the interest of this educational effort, Catherine and a woman named Fanny Tighe traveled to France in 1825 to study the educational system among slum dwellers of that country. Catherine also made close observations of the well-established Kildare Place Schools in Dublin, whose educational standards were excellent, but whose proselytizing techniques were offensive to Catholic families. All the while she dealt with growing controversy about Baggot Street as friends and neighbors became aware of her intent for this residence. To say the least, Catherine's hands were full and her days given over to a variety of tasks in a variety of sites.

When it became apparent that Mary was dying of tuberculosis, Catherine moved into the Macauley household and once more brought her nursing and managerial skills to bear on a situation of need. Her sister's return to the faith of her childhood was reward enough to Catherine. Deference to her husband's strong anti-Catholic sentiments prevented Mary from telling her husband, although she confided the secret to her eldest daughter. After her sister's death, Catherine continued to live for a time in the Macauley home in order to care for her five nieces and nephews.

Dr. Macauley made use of every opportunity to ridicule both her faith and her Baggot Street project. One evening, during a particularly tense exchange on the subject of religion, Catherine let slip the fact of Mary's reconciliation with Catholicism. Enraged, Dr. Macauley stormed from the dining room, apparently in search of his military sword. Catherine fled to a friend's home where Dr. Macauley, apologetic and contrite, called for her the next morning.

Shortly thereafter the Baggot Street building was readied enough for occupants. Catherine's presence was still required in her sister's home, but an acquaintance, Anna Maria Doyle, and Catherine's young charge, Catherine Byrn, moved to the Baggot Street residence and Catherine came daily to assist with the activities there.

Mercy on Baggot Street

Eventually Catherine felt free to join her companions at Baggot Street. Within a short time a coterie of young socialites interested in the education of young working women offered their time, talents, and financial assistance to the works of mercy occurring in the confines of "Kitty's folly." Eventually, this group of companions adopted similar dress and a style of life that to outside observers seemed remarkably conventual.

In these circumstances, encouragement to found a religious order began to come from Daniel Murray, Archbishop of Dublin, and other concerned friends. Catherine struggled with this question over a three-year period, but accepted the recommendation as a way of giving stability to her works. Ultimately she agreed to become the founder of the Sisters of Mercy. Two years before her death, in 1839, Catherine records quite simply the resolution and its impact on her life:

> I would find it most difficult to write what you say Mr.
> Clarke wishes [an account of the beginning of the Order],

for the circumstances which would make it interesting could never be introduced in public discourse. It commenced with 2, Sister Doyle and I. The plan from the beginning was such as is now in practice. In '27 the House was opened. In a year and a half we were joined so fast that it became a matter of general wonder. . . . Seeing us increase so rapidly, and all going on in the greatest order almost of itself, great anxiety was expressed to give it stability. We who began were prepared to do whatever was recommended and in September 1830 we went with Dear Sister Harley to George's Hill to serve a novitiate for the purpose of firmly establishing it. In December '31 we returned and the progress has gone on as you know. (Ignatia Neumann, ed., *Letters of Catherine McAuley*, pp. 154–155)

New Seed and Flower

This beginning described by Catherine McAuley placed her in select company. She joined a small list of persons in the Roman Catholic tradition whose vision not only founded a religious congregation, but also shaped a new form of religious life. In eighteenth- and nineteenth-century Ireland, three remembered for such a contribution are Mary Aikenhead (Irish Sisters of Charity), Nano Nagle (Presentation Sisters), and Catherine McAuley.

In an era when cloistered life was the norm for women in religious congregations, these women struggled, as Angela Merici, Jane deChantal, Louise de Marillac, and Mary Ward had struggled before them, to create apostolic religious life. They hoped to create communities of women actively involved in meeting the needs of God's people. In such communities "vows and common life were ordered to mission, rather than mission being a simple overflow of monastic life" (Sandra Schneiders, "Reflections on the History of Religious Life and Contemporary Development," in *Turning Points in Religious Life*, ed. Carol Quigley, p. 35).

Catherine McAuley, Nano Nagle, and Mary Aikenhead benefited from their circumstances within an Irish culture possessing a rich history that recognized the gifts of women in social and political life. Even so, Catherine's hope to gather a band of women who might serve the needs of the poor in the name of the church was not easily realized. Social mores relative to women's place in the world order as well as an ecclesial atmosphere that favored cloister for women dedicating their lives to the church occasioned subtle but effective resistance. In addition, Catherine struggled with the biases of her own heart, the destructive play of public opinion, and the censorship of clerical colleagues.

Catherine shared the Protestant skepticism about and distaste for the apparently privileged lifestyle of religious congregations. She did not wish to become a member of such a grouping, nor to create that expectation among those who gathered with her to serve Dublin's poor. Her original intent is quite clearly stated in a letter written in September 1828:

> With full approbation of His Grace the Archbishop, the institution in Baggot Street is to go according to the original intention. Ladies who prefer a conventual life, and are prevented embracing it from the nature of property or connections, may retire to this house. It is expected a gratuity will be given and an annual pension paid sufficient to meet the expense a lady must incur. (Angela Bolster, ed., *The Correspondence of Catherine McAuley, 1827–1841*, p. 2)

She also experienced fierce opposition to women taking on leadership in the church. Such opposition expressed in a variety of ways began to suggest a possible value in official approval. A recent biography of Catherine McAuley describes one such instance recorded in a Dublin manuscript:

> [Rev. Matthias Kelly] had no great idea that the unlearned sex could do anything but mischief by trying to assist the clergy. Furthermore, he was prejudiced against [Catherine] whom he considered as *parvenue*. His opinions, perhaps, influenced the curates by whom he was greatly loved; for certainly they did not affect to be glad of the establishment [of the House of Mercy] either as a secular or religious institute. (Bolster, *In Her Own Words*, p. 34)

Gradually, Catherine began to understand the importance of ecclesial approval for the stabilization of her work on behalf of poor persons. For the sake of this work, she yielded to the advice of many friends and colleagues, especially Archbishop Murray. Arrangements were made with the Presentation Sisters in Dublin to provide a novitiate experience for the newly organizing religious congregation.

Catherine McAuley, fifty-two-year-old heiress, foster mother, and administrator, entered her novitiate at George's Hill in September 1830. Two younger women, Anna Maria Doyle and Elizabeth Harley, entered with her. Records indicate that no special privileges were accorded the age or station of Miss McAuley. In fact, she may well have been tested more severely than her youthful companions. All of them suffered great anxiety of heart as their novitiate year drew to a close and the Presentation Sisters began to question the appropriateness of their taking vows for a congregation not yet approved by the church. Archbishop Murray came to the rescue in this instance, and, on 12 December 1831, the newly professed religious returned to Baggot Street amid great rejoicing.

Baggot Street House was designated the first Convent of Mercy the next day, and Catherine was installed as Mother Superior. Still very reluctant to take on the trappings of religious life as currently expressed, Catherine wished not to use the title "Reverend Mother." The Archbishop insisted. They compromised. Catherine would accept the title "Mother Catherine," and the title would be used when necessary. An early companion observed that "what pleased us most in Reverend Mother McAuley was the absence of a manner telling: 'I am the Foundress'" (Bertrand Degnan, *Mercy Unto Thousands: Life of Mother Mary Catherine McAuley, Foundress of the Sisters of Mercy*, p. 246).

Foundations

Whatever her manner may have conveyed, the reality of the role of founder became more and more evident. Activities of service multiplied as well as the number of volunteers seeking to join the endeavors, permanently or temporarily.

Practical programs were established to prepare the residents of the House of Mercy on Baggot Street for employment and self-sufficiency. An employment agency placed young women trained in domestic skills in the homes of reputable families. A laundry staffed by the residents provided much needed income for the works of mercy. Messages delivered for payment supported young orphan boys.

An annual bazaar featured handiwork of residents and renowned personages. Princess Victoria, soon to be queen, donated decorated boxes on one occasion, and the daughters of the Liberator, Irish nationalist Daniel O'Connell, contributed time and talent from the beginning. The Liberator himself once carved the turkey for Christmas dinner at Baggot Street. While some considered the ways of Catherine McAuley inappropriately forthright and assertive, many others eagerly joined forces in her multiple efforts to address the needs of Dublin's slum dwellers.

In 1832 a cholera epidemic spread suffering and death throughout Dublin. The Sisters from Baggot Street spent long hours in the Cholera Hospital. Catherine would recall for future novices the memory of the Sisters returning shortly after nine in the evening, loosening their cinctures on the stairs, and stopping, overcome by sleep before reaching the next floor. Because the great haste to be rid of diseased bodies often resulted in premature burial, Catherine herself inspected those thought dead to ensure that this was indeed the case.

The news of the Sisters' labor and other works of the "Baggot Street Ladies" soon spread to other sections of the capital city and to points beyond. Requests began to arrive at Baggot Street for the establishment of similar Houses of Mercy in other places in Ireland, England, and eventually, the New World. Between 1831 and her death in 1841, Catherine McAuley's fledgling congregation was responsible for fourteen foundations: twelve in Ireland and two in England. The request to establish a foundation in Newfoundland was delayed until after her death.

Death from tuberculosis and cholera as well as calls for new foundations depleted the ranks of early Sisters at Baggot Street and elsewhere, but Catherine seemed always ready "to divide [whatever she had], be it ever so little" (*Letters*, p. 353).

Often, too, dwindling ranks seemed to attract new entrants almost in proportion to the increase in demands for service. Catherine's trust in a providential God was rarely challenged in this regard, although the circumstances of many early foundations strained both trust and courage on all sides.

Kingstown, the first foundation outside Dublin, was the source of both humor and heartbreak. A misunderstanding between Catherine and the parish priest concerning the payment of the bills for the construction of a school left Catherine the focus of a lawsuit. "I am," she wrote in a letter to her dear friend, Sr. M. Frances Warde, "hiding from some law person who wants to serve a paper on me personally. . . . I am afraid to remain five minutes in the small parlor. This has caused more laughing than crying, for every man is suspected of being the process man, and kept at an awful distance" (*Letters*, p. 116).

Travel to the Charleville foundation in 1836 in itself proved trying. The trip from Dublin required canal packet boat to Tullamore, where the pilgrims transferred to a connecting packet that was delayed until midnight. After twenty hours on the canal, they transferred again in Limerick, this time to stagecoach, reaching Charleville the next morning. Once there, they found the house not quite ready for their arrival and so damp that their clothes did not dry out overnight.

Anglo-Irish animosity and Catholic-Protestant prejudices surrounded their foundations in England. English newspapers decried the proposed establishment of the convent in Bermondsey to such an extent that mob activity was feared. Although no public demonstrations actually attended their arrival, discomforts of culture and climate marked each step of the journey. During the process of settling the young community at Birmingham, the last of her foundations, Catherine began to show clear signs of the imminent approach of her death.

The Bloom Fades

Catherine wrote from Birmingham to the infirmarian at Baggot Street requesting some preparations for her return there.

A week later, another letter to Mary Aloysius Scott in Birr began with the comment: "I have been very weak and sick for the past twelve or fourteen days. . . . Endless visitors coming in here and I cannot leave the one aired room without coughing violently" (*Letters*, pp. 373–374).

On her return to Baggot Street, her sorrowing colleagues perceived that she was in her last illness. Catherine inconspicuously settled her private affairs, saw to the ordering of community business, and calmly turned her attention to the journey of death. To Elizabeth Moore, who had traveled from Limerick when informed of Catherine's condition, fell the task of informing the community of her death. She wrote simply: "'Of our dear Reverend Mother what shall I say? or what can I say but that she died the death of the just'" (Savage, *Catherine McAuley*, p. 376).

Perennial Harvest

In her dying, Catherine generated an abundant harvest that grafted to the ancient stock of the works of mercy a new shoot that combined action and contemplation, common life and vows shaped by service. Catherine's petition to the Holy See in 1833 clearly maintains her intent that the congregation she founded be dedicated to service outside convent walls:

> The principle aim of this Congregation is to educate poor girls, to lodge and maintain poor young women who are in danger . . . and to visit the sick poor. (*Correspondence*, p. 12)

The priority of that service in shaping common life and vows continued to be her clear intent in a letter Catherine wrote to the Vicar-Apostolic in the Midlands District of England on the occasion of the last foundation in her lifetime:

> I give you a copy of our distribution of time . . . which has been found well-adapted to the duties of our Order. It is contained in our observances, not in our Rule, and therefore subject to any alteration that place or circumstances might require. (*Correspondence*, p. 161)

The congregation founded by Catherine McAuley has continued to bear fruit through years of service to God's people.

Catherine's Spirituality

Perhaps Catherine's greatest contribution to the church, however, is not the congregation itself as much as the spirituality that enlivened it—a fresh and fertile blending of the contemplative spirit and the compassionate heart. This blending of contemplative spirit and compassionate heart unique to the early Mercy community was a gift not equally prized nor understood. For instance, when Clare Agnew became superior in Bermondsey her "extremes in piety" (*Letters*, p. 354), manifested in part by her desire to establish perpetual adoration in the convent, evoked from Catherine a clear articulation of the essential interplay between prayer and ministry in the life of a Sister of Mercy.

> We should often reflect that our progress in Spiritual Life consists in the faithful discharge of the duties belonging to our state, as regards both ourselves and our neighbour; we must consider the time and exertion which we employ for the relief and instruction of the poor and ignorant as most conducive to our own advancement in perfection, and the time given to prayer and all other pious exercises, etc., we must consider as employed to obtain the grace, strength and animation which alone could enable us to persevere in the meritorious obligations of our state. . . . We must try to be like those rivers which enter into the sea, without losing any of the sweetness of the water." (*Correspondence*, pp. 242–243)

This spirituality which is both rooted in the practical concerns of our needy world and growing faithfully toward greater union with God is succinctly described in the *Positio*:

> Her "spirituality was marked by her ability to create and maintain inner spiritual space, to be constantly aware of the mystery of God and to be able to find His touch

everywhere in the world of people, of their occupations and of their miseries. . . . Her apostolic spirituality may be said to have effectively translated the Gospel into the idiom of her time and to have conveyed this ideal to others." (Pp. 830–831)

Catherine's understanding that the authentic living of the Gospel calls us deeply into relationship with God and into the realities of our time has continued to flower among her Sisters and among all those whose experience of God opens their heart to the world's needs.

In particular, Catherine's spirituality formed itself around several key themes:

Nourishing Prayer

Catherine experienced the life of prayer to which she felt herself called and to which she called her companions as both gift and responsibility: "'Of all other gifts, [the gift of] prayer must come from God; hence we must beg it continually'" (Bolster, *Positio*, p. 782). She cautioned the sisters: "'Prayer is a plant, the seed of which is sown in the heart of every Christian, but its growth depends on the care we take to nourish it. If neglected, it will die. If nourished by constant practice, it will blossom and produce fruit in abundance'" (Bolster, *Positio*, p. 782).

This life of prayer was firmly rooted in the Gospel and in the traditional spirituality of her day. At the center of this spirituality was the person of Jesus Christ. The Psalter of Jesus, the Eucharist, the Passion, and the Sacred Heart were her favorite devotions; the desire to imitate Jesus was her constant yearning.

Mercy

Just as Catherine fostered within the church a new expression of religious life, she nurtured a spirituality suited to that new expression. A ministry responsive to the suffering of the world must be nourished by a prayer that not only strengthens our union with God, but impels us to a practical outpouring of love for God's people:

Prayer, retirement and recollection are not sufficient for those who are called to labor for the salvation of souls. They should be . . . as the compass that goes round its circle without stirring from its center. Now, our center is God from Whom all our actions should spring as from their source. (Teresa Purcell, *Retreat Instructions of Mother Mary Catherine McAuley*, p. 154)

For Catherine, prayer and ministry were not separate experiences but two dimensions of the one vocation revealing God's mercy among the suffering people she met each day. Prayer, "constant fervent prayer" (Angela Bolster, *Catherine McAuley: Venerable for Mercy*, p. 40), was the source of the "grace, strength and animation," without which "all . . . efforts would be fruitless" (*Letters*, p. 385).

Catherine exhorted the sisters to "consider the time and exertion [employed] for the relief and instruction of the poor and ignorant as most conducive to [their] own advancement in perfection" (*Letters*, p. 385). She promised that they could expect to meet Jesus among the poor and encouraged them to allow their hearts to be "animated with gratitude and love" as persons whom Christ "has graciously permitted to assist him in the person of his suffering poor" (Rule 3:15).

A Playful and Grateful Spirit

While Catherine's spirituality drew her into the midst of the world's suffering, her deep, abiding confidence in God's love and protection engendered a playful spirit. Because she knew that God would soon come "both hands filled with favors and blessings" (*Letters*, p. 204), she was able to cast even difficult experiences in a humorous light. This playfulness often expressed itself in verse. When Mary Ann Doyle developed an inflammation of the knees from crawling from bed to bed nursing cholera victims, Catherine penned this poem to lift her spirits:

Dear Sister Doyle, accept from me
for your poor suffering martyrs,
a Laurel Wreath to crown each knee
in place of former garters.

Since fatal Cholera appeared,
you've scarce been seen to stand:
nor danger to yourself e'er feared,
when death o'erspread the land.

While on your knees from bed to bed
you quickly moved about,
it did not enter in your head
that *knees could e'er wear out!*

You've hurt the marrow to the bone,
imploring aid and pity;
and every Cardinal in Rome
would say you saved the City.

Now that the story of your fame
in Annals may be seen:
we'll give each wounded knee a name—
CHOLERA and CHOLERENE!

(*Correspondence*, p. 10)

Catherine's deep trust in God's goodness strengthened her and helped her cope, with a playful and grateful spirit, with the many trials that faced her.

Cordial Love

Perhaps the most tender and telling example of Catherine's spirit is the "comfortable cup of tea" that she asked to have prepared for the Sisters watching at her deathbed. This simple, loving gesture has served, for generations of Sisters of Mercy, as an illustration of the generous and hospitable manner in which she opened herself to her God, her Sisters, and the suffering poor who were so dear to her heart. In the meditations that follow, the image of a comfortable cup of tea will serve as an invitation to enter a comfortable, centered space in which to meet oneself and our gracious God.

Catherine for Today

In a world yearning for the touch of mercy, Catherine's example may be both encouraging and empowering. She had no great design, only a desire to make some lasting effort for God's poor. This yearning engendered a response that was practical and immediate, warm and cordial, enabling and respectful. Through this personal and simple approach, she invites us to walk in the path of mercy, the principal path marked out for those who wish to follow Jesus.

✧ Meditation 1 ✧

The Principal Path: Mercy

Theme: Having experienced the mercy of God, Catherine transformed her gratitude into acts of mercy performed for others. She called mercy "the principal path pointed out by Jesus Christ to those who are desirous of following him" (Regan and Keiss, *Tender Courage*, p. 46).

Opening prayer: Merciful God, open my eyes and ears to the misery around me; open my hands and heart in generous and compassionate response. Through my compassion for those in need, may your mercy be known in our world.

About Catherine

When it was learned that the work at Baggot Street would be completed in time for the house to open on 24 September 1827, the feast of Our Lady of Mercy, Anna Maria Doyle suggested that Mercy be the name placed over the door. And so it was.

Although naming the house Mercy was not Catherine McAuley's idea, her ministry to people in need—whether taking care of poor children, nursing sick people, or sheltering women—was doing the spiritual and corporal works of mercy. From her youth until her death, mercy was Catherine's pathway to Christ. The story of her last foundation illustrates the centrality of mercy in her spirituality.

In December 1840, Catherine established a foundation in the town of Birr, where a Father Crotty, declaring that "nothing is to be feared but popery," had led a number of the townspeople into schism (*Letters*, p. 286). The Sisters of Mercy had been invited to establish a community in Birr in the hopes that their presence would help restore both the faith of the people and peace in the community. In her letters from Birr, Catherine describes the schismatics as "poor Crottyites . . . most unhappy, tho' still obstinate" (*Letters*, p. 286).

Her first visitation was to an old couple whose only son had recently been killed in a fall. Catherine and her companion walked a mile and a half through the snow to offer consolation and to speak to the couple about their religion. Shortly after their arrival, a "Crottyite Lady" arrived, obviously to end any talk of religion. Undaunted, Catherine moved her chair close to the fire and prepared to wait her out. Eventually the woman left, and the conversation continued.

Catherine did not chide or condemn the old couple, but tried to instruct them. Having earlier in her own life felt unequipped to defend her faith, she began to offer the couple insights that would help them make better judgment about the teachings of Father Crotty. Her sympathy for their losses— both of their son and of their faith—moved her to respond to them compassionately and practically. Practical also was her assessment of the outcome of her visit: "They both promised to come to us, but I fear they have been too long in a perverse state to hope that one visit would produce effect" (*Letters*, pp. 287–288).

Catherine concluded her description of this experience with an exclamation welling up from her merciful spirit and revealing her anguish for the plight of the schismatics: "What an awful thing is the loss of Grace, a perverse spirit seems to hold the heart and force it on to ruin" (*Letters*, p. 288).

Pause: Prepare a comfortable cup of tea and think of a time in your own life when you experienced God's compassionate and practical love.

Catherine's Words

Sweet Mercy!—soothing, patient, kind—
softens the high and rears the fallen mind;
knows with just rein and even hand to guide
between false fear and arbitrary pride.
Not easily provoked, she soon forgives:
feels love for all, and by a look, relieves.
Soft peace she brings wherever she arrives,
removes our anguish and reforms our lives;
makes the rough paths of peevish nature even,
and opens in each heart a little heaven.

(Bolster, *Positio*, p. 817)

Reflection

Carmel Bourke, a biographer of Catherine, reminds us of
Thomas Aquinas's definition of mercy: "A heart suffering over
the sufferings of others" (Bourke, *A Woman Sings of Mercy*,
p. 48). Though this word and its definition fit perfectly both
Catherine's spirit and her manner of being in the world, it was
not one of her choosing. As noted, Anna Marie Doyle named
the house on Baggot Street "Mercy." However, Catherine felt
drawn to mercy as "the principal path" for those who want to
follow Jesus.

The events of her own life helped her know God's loving
care and providence. Remembering God's tender mercy for
her in moments of pain, loss, and uncertainty, she committed
herself and her resources to making God's love tangible and
practical in the lives of Dublin's poor. Catherine recognized a
distinction between charity and mercy. Both arise from the
heart, but mercy requires a more personal response. She once
remarked: "'The mercy of God comes to our assistance and
renders practical His love in our regard'" (Bolster, *Positio*,
p. 817).

Catherine knew mercy to be a demanding virtue. To take
into one's heart the misery of another, to humbly accept one's
limitations in the face of suffering and need, and to know that
attentive love is sometimes all one has to offer demand

courage and, of course, God's boundless grace. Nevertheless, following in the footsteps of Jesus, Catherine called herself, her Sisters, and her associates to follow the pathway of mercy.

✧ Make a list of instances in your own life when you have experienced God's merciful and active love. How can you turn these experiences into mercy for others?

✧ Slowly read the "Catherine's Words" section again, pondering the passage's meaning for you. Which of the qualities of mercy that she describes do you most need God's grace to acquire? Ask Jesus for the grace you need to be more merciful.

✧ Read the Sermon on the Mount in Matthew, chapters 5, 6, and 7, and Luke, chapter 6. What instances of God's practical love can you find in these passages? What challenges do you find in the exhortation to be merciful as God is merciful? Pray for the courage to meet these challenges.

✧ In the Book of Exodus, God frequently reminds the Hebrew people that they should be good to strangers, widows, and orphans because they had been strangers in the land of Egypt until God brought them out. Who are the stranger, the widow, and the orphan in our contemporary society, in your neighborhood, in your family? How can you be part of God's saving love for them?

✧ Identify "the stranger, the widow, and the orphan" within yourself. What acts of practical mercy can you extend to yourself? Are you able to graciously receive the mercy of others?

✧ Volunteer for an organization that has as its focus the alleviation of some manifestation of the world's misery.

God's Word

From the beginning, this is the message that you have heard: love one another.

Proof of God's love for us is that Jesus sacrificed his life for us. In our turn, we ought to sacrifice our life for our sisters and brothers. For instance, if you are wealthy in the goods of this world and see people in want and shut your heart to them, how can you possibly think that love of God lives within you? Our love must be more than hollow words. It must be authentic and take action. (Adapted from 1 John 3:11–18)

Closing prayer:

My God
I am Yours
for time and eternity.
Teach me to cast myself entirely
into the arms of
Your loving Providence
with the most lively, unlimited
confidence in Your
compassionate, tender pity.
Grant me,
O most merciful Redeemer,
that whatever
You ordain or permit
may be acceptable to me.
Take from my heart all painful anxiety;
suffer nothing to sadden me but sin,
nothing to delight me but the hope
of coming to the possession of You,
my God and my all,
in Your everlasting Kingdom.
Amen.

(Catherine McAuley)

✧ Meditation 2 ✧

Hearts Centered in God, Presence, and Prayer

Theme: Catherine nurtured a steady awareness of God's presence in daily experience through frequent exercises of piety and participation in sacramental rituals.

Opening prayer: Incarnate God, you are present in my person and in my experience. Eyes that seek and ears that listen detect daily wonder. May my eyes and ears always be open to such discovery.

About Catherine

Through her long years as a caretaker, housekeeper, and member of Dublin's social set, Catherine McAuley had cultivated a steady awareness of God's presence in her everyday experience. Some time after her father's death, Catherine copied in childish script the Psalter of Jesus to be recited often during the day. As a young woman at Coolock House, she used natural objects to lift her heart to God: the cross in the branches of trees, in the window frames, and in door panels of the house. This quiet centeredness in God sustained Catherine in the whirlwind of activity that marked the fourteen years between the founding of the House of Mercy in Dublin in 1827 and her death in 1841.

Because it was her custom to accompany the women appointed to establish new houses for the works of mercy, these years of foundation were filled with the hustle and bustle of travel. Catherine and the Sisters opened eleven houses in Ireland and two in England. In numerous journeys, alone and with companions, Catherine traversed land and sea, by coach and canal boat, in good weather and bad, with many mishaps and hardships.

In her last year and already ill with the sickness that would soon claim her life, Catherine was nevertheless determined to undertake the journey to Birmingham, England, to establish a new foundation. Correspondence written in the months between the planning and the establishment of this foundation (June–September 1841) gives hints of her fatigue. She wrote to her friend Sr. M. Frances Warde: "I have really got a surfeit [of travel]" (p. 232). In other letters, she begins with a reference to her hurrying: "I have only ten minutes now" (p. 234); "I could not get half-an-hour till this moment to write to you" (p. 254); and "I write in haste" (*Correspondence*, p. 259).

The pace seemed to ease very little once travel began: "We had our ceremony on Thursday and sailed on Friday; got here about four o'clock on Saturday; had scarcely time to [change] when we were summoned to the choir" (*Correspondence*, p. 254). Even so, Catherine took time to write to friends, business acquaintances, and coworkers.

In the midst of all the activity and in spite of her ill health, she sums up her firm faith in the sustaining role of prayer in a letter to Sr. Aloysius Scott: "Prayer will do more [to solving our difficulties] . . . than all the money in the Bank of Ireland. Let us pray well and never grow weary" (*Letters*, p. 349).

Pause: Prepare a comfortable cup of tea and think of a story from your own life that reflects your awareness of God present in the midst of the busyness of life.

Catherine's Words

We have one solid comfort amidst this little tripping about, our hearts can always be in the same place, centered in God, for whom alone we go forward or stay back. Oh, may God look on us with love and pity and then we shall be able to do anything He wishes us to do, no matter how difficult to accomplish or painful to our feelings. (*Letters*, p. 273)

If the love of God really reigns in your heart, it will quickly show itself in the exterior. You will become sweet and attractive in manner. You will have a tender esteem . . . for everyone, beholding in them the image of God. (Purcell, *Retreat Instructions*, p. 145)

Reflection

The *Positio*, written in preparation for the cause of canonization, describes Catherine McAuley as "alive to the power of God" and "firmly within the ascetical and mystical tradition of the Irish Church" (pp. 775–776). The mystical tradition of her Celtic roots helped Catherine to uncover the divine in everyday reality. Her lifelong devotion to the Eucharist, the Sacred Heart, the Passion, and the Blessed Virgin Mary rooted her prayer in the universal practice of the church.

Catherine the contemplative was also the entrepreneur who created a social service center, laundry, and vocational school for women. She facilitated the establishment of thirteen centers of service in Ireland and England. She mentored and acted as spiritual guide for countless persons who joined her efforts to address suffering and oppression. Catherine was nurse, teacher, administrator, fund-raiser, writer, traveler, and advocate. Yet a remarkable number of personal recollections about Catherine refer to her serenity, unhurried manner, undistracted presence, tranquillity, and peacefulness.

Catherine established a rhythm of God-consciousness through two practices found in many religious traditions: repetition of words and repetition of rituals. Catherine frequently repeated aspirations (short prayers of petition and praise) found in the Psalter of Jesus and in other sources of Catholic devotion. She also participated regularly in eucharistic celebrations and celebrations of the sacrament of reconciliation. As her spiritual advice to people suggests, Catherine realized that a habit of awareness is a matter of discipline, of regular and deliberate effort. Awareness of God's presence and our response in prayer give grounding, focus, and strength to do God's works of mercy.

✦ Practice centering prayer. Sit very still. Breathe slowly and deliberately. If other thoughts come to mind, just let them float away. Focus the energy of your being on the repetition of one word such as *God, mercy, love,* or *Jesus.* Gradually let the word make its home in you.

Select a short phrase or prayer to repeat throughout the day. Be aware of the effect this repetition may have on your thoughts, attitudes, and actions. Occasionally ask yourself how this practice of simple prayer changes the quality of your day.

✦ Watch an athlete or an artist at work. Observe the focus of his or her energy toward their purpose. Notice the manner in which he or she silences all that does not pertain to that purpose. What can we who wish to develop the art or skill of prayer learn from such persons?

✦ Select a scene from the Gospels: for example, Jesus' curing the lepers, raising the young boy of Nain, or speaking to the Canaanite woman. Imagine the noise and activity of the scene. Study the movements of the different persons. Describe the manner of Jesus' presence to these people.

✦ Allow the busyness of your day to be an occasion of prayer. Pause after each phone conversation to commend the caller to God. Pray for people around you in a traffic jam. Pray for the service station attendant, supermarket checker, bus driver, letter carrier, and delivery person. Pray for the ability to be a peaceful presence in the world each time you go out your door. At the end of each day, ask yourself: How did this practice change the quality of my day?

God's Word

In the morning, long before dawn, [Jesus] got up and left the house and went off to a lonely place and prayed there. Simon and his companions set out in search of him, and when they found him they said, "Everybody is looking for you." He answered, "Let us go elsewhere, to the neighbouring country towns, so that I can proclaim the message there too, because that is why I came." And he went all through Galilee, preaching in their synagogues and driving out devils. (Mark 1:35–39)

Closing prayer:

My God
I am Yours
for time and eternity.
Teach me to cast myself entirely
into the arms of
Your loving Providence
with the most lively, unlimited
confidence in Your
compassionate, tender pity.
Grant me,
O most merciful Redeemer,
that whatever
You ordain or permit
may be acceptable to me.
Take from my heart all painful anxiety;
suffer nothing to sadden me but sin,
nothing to delight me but the hope
of coming to the possession of You,
my God and my all,
in Your everlasting Kingdom.
Amen.

(Catherine McAuley)

✧ Meditation 3 ✧

Trust in the Faithful Provider

Theme: For Catherine, the providence of God was revealed in the ordinary experiences of life. Trust in this providence engendered in both serenity and hope.

Opening prayer: Provident God, open my eyes to see the evidence of your caring love in daily life. Help me to recognize in persons and events, and in the unfolding design of my life, the revelations of your goodness.

About Catherine

Originally William Callaghan had intended to divide his estate equally between Catherine McAuley and Mary Ann Powell, a cousin of Mrs. Callaghan. However, Mr. Callaghan overheard Mary Ann's husband describing changes that would be made when his wife inherited the Callaghan home, Coolock House. Among these, he envisioned restricting Catherine's religious associations. Offended by the bigotry inherent in Powell's remarks, Mr. Callaghan added a codicil to his will naming Catherine as his sole heir. This unexpected benefaction provided Catherine with the resources needed to stabilize her ministry to poor people. Catherine naturally attributed this unexpected additional beneficence to God's loving providence.

Catherine's confidence in her "faithful provider" continued to be a source of serenity and hope throughout her life. For instance, like so many of the foundations, the beginnings of Tullamore were fragile from a financial perspective. Nevertheless, Catherine encouraged the first superior, Mary Ann Doyle, to "have the most strong and lively confidence that your convent will be firmly established for it certainly will." She went on to encourage her not to be deterred by temporal considerations, but to offer the Sisters' services "most freely and relying with unhesitating confidence on the Providence of God" (*Letters*, pp. 352–353).

This same letter revealed Catherine's appreciation for the evidences of this reliance on providence in her sisters. She shared with Mary Ann Doyle the story of an applicant to the order whose mother was concerned for her security and questioned the wisdom of handing over all that she possessed. The applicant's mother questioned what her daughter would do should the order not survive. The daughter replied, "Won't I have my sweet Lord?" Catherine comments: "Though we may not often have the consolation to meet such noble universal disengagement as hers, yet, a spirit, directly opposite, I humbly hope will never make its abode among us" (p. 353).

The last day of her life revealed how consistently and deeply she trusted her "faithful provider." Frances Gibson, soon to be superior of the founding community in Liverpool, expressed her anguish about the loss of Catherine's guidance. "'Mother, don't leave us! What will the congregation do if you die?'" Catherine's response was simple and direct: "'If the Order be my work, the sooner it falls to the ground the better. If it is God's work, it needs no one'" (Bourke, *A Woman Sings of Mercy*, pp. 71–72).

Pause: Prepare a comfortable cup of tea and consider the ordinary circumstances of your life that might reveal the guidance of a providential God.

Catherine's Words

[The Congregation of Mercy] commenced with 2, Sister Doyle and I. The plan from the beginning was such as is now in practice. In '27 the House was opened. In a year and a half we were joined so fast that it became a matter of general wonder. . . . We now have gone beyond 100 in number, and the desire to join seems rather to increase, though it was thought the foundations would retard it, it seems to be quite otherwise. There has been a most marked Providential Guidance which the want of prudence, vigilance, or judgment has not impeded, and it is here that we can most clearly see the designs of God. I could mark circumstances calculated to defeat it at once, but nothing however injurious in itself has done any injury. This is all I could say.

The loss of property has been supplied, the Death of the most valuable Sisters passed away as of no consequence. The alarm that was spread by such repeated deaths did not prevent others crowding in, in short, it evidently was to go on, and surmount all obstacles, many of which were great indeed, proceeding from causes within and without. (*Letters*, pp. 154–155)

Reflection

Catherine's life was marked by personal and familial tragedies that might have led her to despair that *anyone* cared for her, let alone a God of love and tenderness. Her life contained few extraordinary signs of divine intervention. Yet she cultivated an attentiveness to the subtle signs of God's care and love that flowered in a life characterized by hope and serenity.

Catherine took seriously God's promises of fidelity to us. God never left the Israelites forsaken. The Faithful Provider sent Jesus the Christ to save each of us. Jesus told us to ask for what we need. The care of our benevolent God is revealed in the ordinary and extraordinary events of life. Often we only understand the workings of God's providence in hindsight, but when we reflect on the patterns in our life, we can see God's hand. Attentiveness to the past acts of providence and to what is happening now calls us to deepen our faith and trust in the presence and providence of God.

✧ Reflect on obvious instances of God's provident care in your life. How is this care mediated through persons, places, or events? How did you come to recognize God's presence in these instances? Does your experience verify Catherine's observation that God is a faithful provider?

✧ Look deeply into the ordinary circumstances of your life, especially the last several days. What do you find of God's provident love in these ordinary circumstances? Pause to be grateful for the subtlety of God's care.

✧ Generosity, from Catherine's perspective, consists not solely in giving material gifts, but in the impulse to "bestow ourselves most freely and rely with unhesitating confidence on the Providence of God." Are there instances when your experience of God's providence has enabled you to risk bestowing yourself "most freely"? Ponder these times, and discuss them with your Faithful Provider.

✧ Just as William Callaghan was God's providential instrument, we are invited to manifest God's providence—to be Faithful Providers—by the care we give to our sisters and brothers. If only in a simple act of kind, unexpected service, expend yourself for someone today.

God's Word

"Think of the ravens. They do not sow or reap; they have no storehouses and no barns; yet God feeds them. And how much more you are worth than the birds! Can any of you, however much you worry, add a single cubit to your span of life? If a very small thing is beyond your powers, why worry about the rest? Think how the flowers grow; they never have to spin or weave; yet, I assure you, not even Solomon in all his royal robes was clothed like one of them. Now if that is how God clothes a flower which is growing wild today and is thrown into the furnace to-morrow, how much more will [God] look after you! . . . There is no need to be afraid, little flock, for it has pleased [God] to give you the kingdom." (Luke 12:24–32)

Closing prayer:

My God,
I am Yours
for time and eternity.
Teach me to cast myself entirely
into the arms of
Your loving Providence
with the most lively unlimited
confidence in Your
compassionate, tender pity.
Grant me,
O most merciful Redeemer,
that whatever
You ordain or permit
may be acceptable to me.
Take from my heart all painful anxiety;
suffer nothing to sadden me, but sin,
nothing to delight me but the hope
of coming to the possession of You,
my God and my all,
in Your everlasting Kingdom.
Amen.

(Catherine McAuley)

✧ Meditation 4 ✧

Service for God, Not for Thanks

Theme: For Catherine, imitation of Jesus' tender love—especially for poor people—is the heart of the Christian vocation.

Opening prayer:

My God, look down with pity and mercy on your afflicted poor and give [me] the grace to do all I can for their relief and comfort. [I] most humbly ask your blessing this day in the name and for the sake of our Lord and Saviour Jesus Christ. (Bolster, *Positio*, p. 818)

About Catherine

Although Catherine's father died when she was quite young, her memories of his caring response to poor people were a guiding influence in her life. On Sundays and holidays, James McAuley gathered the poor children of the neighborhood in order to instruct them in their religion.

Stories of Catherine's own response to poor people permeate every phase of her life. In the period following the death of the Callaghans, she often visited the poor in their homes. On one such occasion, Catherine discovered an old

Protestant woman, Mrs. Harper, who, although previously in comfortable circumstances, had become impoverished. Catherine brought her home to Coolock House and cared for her until her death five years later. The fact that Mrs. Harper was deranged, that she regularly stole or hid things, that she detested soap and water, and that she continually subjected her benefactor—to whom she took a perverse dislike—to abusive language, did not prevent Catherine from treating her with consummate kindness.

Catherine's commitment to service to the poor was so complete that she wrote into the original Rule that no new convent could be established unless it had "certain revenue adequate to its support" because the "Sisters of this Holy Institute are devoted to the poor, from whom they cannot receive any temporal emolument" (12:1).

Pause: Prepare a comfortable cup of tea and think of a story from your own life that reflects your care for the poor.

Catherine's Words

It is for God we serve the poor and not for thanks. (Bolster, *Venerable for Mercy,* p. 44)

Saint Peter Chrysologus compares those who administer spiritual and corporal aid to the nurses of princes, as he says great care is taken that the nurses of kings' children be supplied with whatever will strengthen and cherish them, so the King of Kings takes care that those who attend to the care of His most dear poor, to whom He is Father, shall be nourished and animated . . . that they may the better fulfill an office so dear to His Paternal heart. We may then truly say to these poor objects of our care what Saint Paul said to the Philippians and Thessalonians, "You are my joy and my crown." (*Letters,* pp. 388–389)

There are three things which the poor prize more highly than gold, tho' they cost the donor nothing; among these are the kind word, the gentle, compassionate look, and the patient hearing of their sorrows. (*Familiar Instructions of Rev. Mother McAuley,* p. 138)

Reflection

Catherine McAuley looked upon service of the poor as both a privilege and an opportunity. She reminded those who were "graciously permitted to assist [Christ] in the person of [the] suffering poor," that their hearts should be "animated with gratitude and love" (Rule 3:15). She told the Sisters that "we should expect to meet our Divine Redeemer in the homes of the poor" (*Familiar Instructions*, p. 18).

The hallmark of her service was her respect for the dignity of each person. Her delicacy in offering assistance, lest the recipients be embarrassed at their need, brought a quality of tenderness and gentility to her practical actions in behalf of the poor. The urgency of her concern made her relentless in her efforts to relieve the effects of poverty, illness, and lack of education.

She reminded the people of her time and reminds us now that service to our poor sisters and brothers is fundamental to loving Christ. By serving them, we serve him.

✧ Read again Catherine's description of the three things prized by the poor in the "Catherine's Words" section. Who are the persons to whom you can offer these "treasures"?

✧ Reflect on the opportunities you have had to interact with persons who are poor. What have these persons taught you about God? About yourself?

✧ In addition to direct service and personal relationships, another way to walk with the poor is through advocacy. Become informed about programs that especially affect the poor and become active in the political process in their behalf.

✧ Think of a poor person with whom you have had some interaction. What three "prizes" did that person offer you?

✧ Pray with the scriptural passages reflecting Jesus' love for the poor. What learnings are there here for you? What incentives are there for practical action on behalf of the poor?

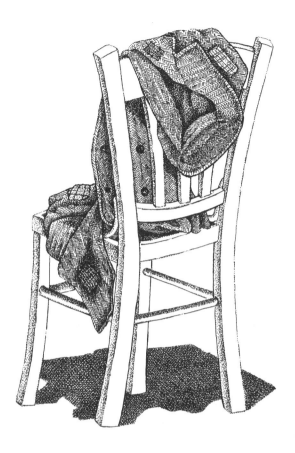

God's Word

No distinctions based on class should be part of your faith in Christ. Imagine that a person walks into the synagogue finely dressed and then a poor person enters in rags. Your standards are all wrong if you say to the rich person, "Take this seat; it's the best one," and you say to the poor person, "You'll have to stand back over there" or "Take a seat on the floor."

Listen, God selected the poor by the world's standards to have a rich faith and to receive the grand inheritance promised to those who love God. (Adapted from James 2:1–5)

Closing prayer:

My God,
I am Yours
for time and eternity.
Teach me to cast myself entirely
into the arms of
Your loving Providence
with the most lively, unlimited
confidence in Your
compassionate, tender pity.
Grant me,
O most merciful Redeemer,
that whatever
You ordain or permit
may be acceptable to me.
Take from my heart all painful anxiety;
suffer nothing to sadden me but sin,
nothing to delight me but the hope
of coming to the possession of You,
my God and my all,
in Your everlasting Kingdom.
Amen.

(Catherine McAuley)

✦ Meditation 5 ✦

Help Today

Theme: Catherine McAuley had no grand design for her ministry, only an urgent desire to care for poor, sick, and uneducated people without delay.

Opening prayer: Servant God, revealed in the mystery of Jesus Christ, open my heart to opportunities to care. Help me to nourish life in small circumstances and global realities. Move me to help those people who need my help today. May I be less concerned with grand plans than with your people in need right now.

About Catherine

At the age of twenty-one, Catherine found herself responsible for her younger siblings and, later, for the children of her recently deceased sister, Mary. She knew firsthand the pain of being housed by others, the constraint of scarce financial resources, and the anxiety of an uncertain future. Catherine learned from these experiences to approach everyone with compassion and gentleness and to preserve the dignity of those in need of assistance.

Shortly after the death of Mrs. Callaghan, a young servant girl from the neighborhood approached Catherine at Coolock House. A man in the household where the girl was employed was pressuring her with unwanted sexual advances. The young woman did not know how she could continue to refuse his advances and appealed for help in her vulnerable circumstance.

Catherine asked a Dublin organization to shelter the young girl until new employment could be found for her away from the neighborhood of her current employer. To her dismay, the organization told Catherine that a committee's approval was necessary for such admission. Her request could not be handled until the next regular board meeting.

Before that gathering was held, the young girl disappeared, never to be seen again. Catherine was beside herself with distress. This incident may have occasioned her oft repeated remark, "'The poor need help today, not next week'" (Bourke, *A Woman Sings of Mercy*, p. 8). She vowed that she would provide against such a circumstance ever happening again. Although it took her several years to accomplish her goal, the House of Mercy built in 1827 was a direct response to this sad story.

Pause: Prepare a comfortable cup of tea and think of a story when someone's immediate need called you to Christian service.

Catherine's Words

It is better to relieve a hundred impostors . . . than to suffer one truly deserving person to be sent away empty. (Bolster, *Venerable for Mercy*, p. 44)

We might often repeat the words of the Psalmist saying: "Teach me goodness, discipline, and knowledge." Goodness first as particularly necessary to incline our hearts to pity for our suffering brethren. Discipline next, that we may so regulate our time and actions as to serve them with zeal and prudence; and knowledge, that we may impart such instruction as will lead them to God, and keep ourselves faithful in our duty. . . . We must try to be like those rivers which enter into the sea, without losing any of the sweetness of the water. We must, in the midst of the rudeness, impiety and impatience which we shall witness, preserve meekness, piety and unwearied patience. . . .

The corporal and spiritual works of mercy . . . so far from separating [us] from the love of God, unite [us] much more closely to Him, and render [us] more valuable in His holy service. (*Letters*, pp. 386–387)

Reflection

Catherine McAuley's desire to serve was rooted in her reading of the Gospels and her desire to imitate Jesus Christ. Even though concern for her family and her neighbors eventually drew her to a concern for the world beyond Baggot Street and Dublin, Catherine knew that poor people needed help immediately and could not always wait for the completion of grand charitable designs.

Personal, often simple, service was a necessary component of her desire to live as Jesus lived. The spontaneous and generous quality of her response to human need is reflected in a comment from Mother Clare Moore, one of Catherine's early companions:

> "The spirit of mercy and compassion for the poor which animated and as it were consumed Rev. Mother, made her sometimes adopt plans for their relief which to some appeared beyond the limits of prudence; but the success with which her undertakings were usually attended showed that she was guided by a heavenly wisdom." (Bourke, *A Woman Sings of Mercy*, p. 79)

All followers of Jesus are called to service. Ministry—an intentional act of service exercised within the Christian tradition in response to human need—is the prerogative of every baptized person. In fact, this conscious choice to respond to the need of another person in Jesus' name remains the distinguishing mark of Christian service.

Christian service may be as simple as giving a cup of water to a thirsty child or as complex as developing a water system for an underdeveloped country. We may offer our energy, talent, money, time—or all of these. How we serve is also important. Jesus and Catherine provide examples of the sort of compassionate, sensitive, cheerful, and generous service that should characterize all Christians.

✦ Identify two or three persons you would name as caring. Try to describe the behaviors and attitudes on which you base your opinion. Do you desire to be more like these people? Ask for the graces you need to become more caring.

✦ Read the Gospel stories of the good Samaritan (Luke 10:29–37), the anointing at Bethany (Mark 14:3–9), the wedding feast at Cana (John 2:1–10), and the cure of the woman bent over (Luke 13:10–17). What characteristics of service are revealed in these portraits?

✦ Think of a time when a situation called out to you so clearly that you were impelled to act with mercy. What was it in this situation that engendered your spontaneous response? What did you learn about yourself in that circumstance?

✦ Review the front page of your local newspaper. Identify systems that serve poor, sick, and uneducated people. Identify systems that burden these people. What did you learn? How were you challenged or called? Pray for the ability to suffer with, to be compassionate.

✦ Identify opportunities for voluntary service in your neighborhood: for example, groups who serve persons who are hungry, persons who are homeless, persons who cannot read. Discern how God calls you to serve through these invitations. Pray to have the courage and energy to act.

God's Word

Jesus proved his love for us when he laid down his life for us. We should be willing to make the same sacrifice. And if we have abundant goods at our disposal, we show our love for God by sharing them generously with our sisters and brothers. Our love has to be real and active.

God is love. We have grown to believe in this love. If you love, God lives in you, and love becomes complete when we can face our final udgment without hesitation because we have imitated Christ's love. (Adapted from 1 John 3:16–18; 4:16–17)

Closing prayer:

My God,
I am Yours
for time and eternity.
Teach me to cast myself entirely
into the arms of
Your loving Providence
with the most lively, unlimited
confidence in Your
compassionate, tender pity.
Grant me,
O most merciful Redeemer,
that whatever
You ordain or permit
may be acceptable to me.
Take from my heart all painful anxiety;
suffer nothing to sadden me but sin,
nothing to delight me but the hope
of coming to the possession of You,
my God and my all,
in Your everlasting Kingdom.
Amen.

(Catherine McAuley)

This Is My Christ

Theme: Catherine's devotion to the Passion of Jesus Christ centered in her realization that daily self-denial constitutes our most transformative imitation of Christ.

Opening prayer: Suffering Servant God, create in me a lively, animated spirit. Help me to appreciate the daily vigilance required to be transformed. Enliven in me a willingness to let go of the tendency to protect myself from the pain of this growth.

About Catherine

Early in her career as founder, a public controversy presented the cross of Christ to Catherine in a shape most distasteful and difficult for her. Through several months, she struggled to engage the situation without resentment and bitterness as a cross she bore for the sake of Christ's people.

The controversy began when Rev. Walter Meyler replaced Rev. Michael Blake as pastor of Saint Andrew's, the parish church of the House of Mercy on Baggot Street. While Reverend Blake was a friend and confidant of Mother McAuley, Reverend Meyler belonged to a small clique of clergy irritated by the activity at Baggot Street. The new pastor found an opportunity to discomfort the upstart McAuley woman, as he viewed her.

When the appointed chaplain of the House of Mercy re-signed, Reverend Meyler had to give approval for a replace-ment. He refused to offer such approval and insisted that the residents of the House of Mercy should walk to Saint An-drew's for daily services. By this time, November 1837, the residents numbered some seventy women, in addition to the women who gathered to serve their needs. The presence of a chaplain provided spiritual counseling for all. In addition, the collection taken up during Mass provided resources needed for the works of mercy. Reverend Meyler's withdrawal of the chaplain embarrassed Catherine, caused financial troubles, and, as Catherine confesses to her friend Sr. M. Frances Warde, was "a smart attack on self-importance" (*Letters*, p. 116).

Had the matter been simply a personal affront, Catherine might well have borne the inconvenience and embarrassment. However, in this application of diocesan regulations, she saw an injustice and inconsistency that placed a burden on many more persons than herself. For these persons and for the sake of justice, Catherine stood her ground.

The resolution came slowly. Catherine wrote one of the Sisters:

> We have just now indeed more than an ordinary portion of the Cross in this one particular, but may it not be the Cross of Christ which we often pray to "be about us"? It has not the marks of an angry Cross, there is no disunion, no gloomy depression of spirits, no departure from char-ity proceeding from it. (*Letters*, p. 115)

After three years of negotiations, a chaplain was restored to the growing population in the House of Mercy on Baggot Street. While this result gratified Catherine, a more important struggle had been going on inside her. "Pray fervently to God to take all bitterness from me," she wrote to Sr. Frances. "I can scarcely think of what has been done to me without resent-ment. May God forgive me and make me humble before He calls me into His presence" (*Letters*, p. 129).

Pause: Prepare a comfortable cup of tea and think of a story from your own life that reflects your understanding of participating in the Passion of Jesus Christ.

Catherine's Words

We seem to forget that God calls upon us to take up our cross and that this cross must be composed of the sacrifice of something that is dear to us, that He requires of us constant watchfulness over our thoughts and words. Is this restraint, this self-denial to make us gloomy, sad or peevish? No, such is not His intention, for it is to the religious loaded with her cross that He has in particular promised the hundredfold, but then this is a conditional promise. It is not made to those who drag their cross after them. . . . No, it is to those who take it up generously, courageously and lovingly. (*Retreat Instructions*, p. 168)

Reflection

Suffering marked Catherine McAuley's life: the early death of her parents, her many years of financial dependence, frequent sickness and death among close acquaintances, opposition to her efforts to help the poor, and separation from those she loved. Catherine herself considered these the ordinary fare of life, sorrows "extensively divided and equally the affliction of many" (*Letters*, p. 100).

When Catherine considered Christ's suffering, the trials and acts of self-sacrifice required in imitating Christ most often came to mind: "What is your cross? When called on to do what is opposed to your judgment, behold your cross! . . . When a harsh or unkind expression is used toward you . . . when anything occurs that is painful to your self-love, behold your cross!" (*Retreat Instructions*, pp. 119–120).

Submitting our heart and will to the ultimate purpose of our creation stands at the center of imitating Christ. The ultimate purpose of our life is, as Saint Paul declared, putting on Christ. Because Christ is love, imitating Christ means putting on love. Love always demands self-sacrifice and often suffering.

In her *Familiar Instructions*, Catherine McAuley records that devotion to the Passion is not a matter of mere sentiment, but must be fruitful in virtues and good works. Imitating

Christ's love will demand self-denial, humility of heart, sweet-ness of manner, and patience in the face of contradictions.

Even so, action alone will not suffice. Saint Paul insists that we must be transformed by renewing our minds, too. Such a transformation requires the daily struggle to embrace the person we are and to grow toward wholeness precisely in that human reality. Living with our humanity means suffering the shadow side of our life even as we rejoice in the bright side. Living with our humanity means seeking to free our-selves of self-centeredness and the biases that prevent a gra-cious acceptance of God's creation. Likewise, it means seeking to overcome the addictions, ignorance, and resistance that ob-struct God's revelation and redemption.

✧ Carefully read each of the Gospel Passion narratives. Reflect on the manner with which Jesus is portrayed by each of the Evangelists as he moves through this experience. What differing nuances can you detect in each portrait? How do these nuances help to complete your understanding of Jesus' Passion experience?

✧ When has love demanded self-sacrifice or suffering for you? Recall times when you embraced the cross of love. Talk with Christ about his Passion and your passion; ask for the graces you need to keep shouldering the crosses of love. Thank God for the beauty and joy of love.

✧ The Scriptures present Simon of Cyrene and Veronica supporting and comforting Jesus during his Passion. Offer some practical gesture of support to a person suffering the passion of illness, alienation, homelessness, or unemployment.

✧ List those qualities that are a part of your bright side and those qualities that are a part of your shadow side. Reflect on the beauty provided in this full picture of your humanity.

✧ Take time today to be conscious of ecological and en-vironmental concerns. Select some action that reflects your ef-fort to join all creation in its yearning to complete its purpose and design.

God's Word

I urge you, then . . . remembering the mercies of God, to offer your bodies as a living sacrifice, dedicated and acceptable to God; that is the kind of worship for you, as sensible people. Do not model your behaviour on the contemporary world, but let the renewing of your minds transform you, so that you may discern for yourselves what is the will of God—what is good and acceptable and mature. (12:1–2)

Pay no regard to social standing, but meet humble people on their own terms. Do not congratulate yourself on your own wisdom. Never pay back evil with evil, but bear in mind the ideals that all regard with respect. As much as is possible, and to the utmost of your ability, be at peace with everyone. (Romans 12:16–18)

Closing prayer:

My God,
I am Yours
for time and eternity.
Teach me to cast myself entirely
into the arms of
Your loving Providence
with the most lively, unlimited
confidence in Your
compassionate, tender pity.
Grant me,
O most merciful Redeemer,
that whatever
You ordain or permit
may be acceptable to me.
Take from my heart all painful anxiety;
suffer nothing to sadden me but sin,
nothing to delight me but the hope
of coming to the possession of You,
my God and my all,
in Your everlasting Kingdom.
Amen.

(Catherine McAuley)

✦ Meditation 7 ✦

Performing the Ordinary, Extraordinarily Well

Theme: Catherine understood that putting on Christ meant doing ordinary deeds with all the love and competence with which God graces us.

Opening prayer: Sustaining God, in whose love all creation yearns to be complete, teach me gentle presence to myself and others. May I live fully one day at a time and love the best that I can through all the ordinary acts of each day.

About Catherine

Catherine McAuley was a prolific letter-writer. These letters were her living link with a sisterhood spreading far and wide even in her lifetime. The letters were chatty, simple renditions of life's ordinary experiences. Topics ran the gamut from congregational tidbits to personal revelations to neighborhood news and stories:

> We have two new Sisters since the ceremony—neither quite twenty, the last we call the Queen, she is exactly her age, an exceedingly nice young person. (P. 159)

The six travellers leave dear Ireland tomorrow—all in tolerable good health and more than tolerable spirits. . . . I have my list of songs prepared for the journey. (Pp. 176–177)

My rather new visitant, a cough, has been with me very constantly since the first Sunday after my return. (*Letters*, p. 311)

The letters always reflect a woman quite alert to the spiritual richness contained in these daily happenings. Writing as the 1841 Lenten season began, Catherine forthrightly counsels Mary deSales White to be practical concerning the Lenten fast: "You will be far more mortified in taking that which you do not like to take, than in abstaining from it. You have not sufficient strength to fast" (*Letters*, p. 310).

In that same letter, Catherine summarizes her sense of doing ordinary actions attentively: "The simplest and most practical lesson I know . . . is to resolve to be good today, but better tomorrow . . . thus we may hope to get on taking short, careful steps, not great strides" (*Letters*, p. 310).

For Catherine, "hope to get on" meant assuming the fundamental task of every Christian to grow daily in love of God and love of neighbor. While always appreciative of the talents of her colleagues, she most often praised kind and generous spirits, sensitive and gentle mannerisms. In her *Retreat Instructions* she asserts quite simply, "If you really love God, you will thus prove your love, for the proof of love is deed. . . . Love of God . . . and love of neighbor . . . are as cause and effect" (p. 147).

Pause: Prepare a comfortable cup of tea and think of a story from your own life that reflects awareness of growing in love "taking short, careful steps."

Catherine's Words

Perfection does not consist in performing extraordinary actions, but rather in performing extraordinarily well the ordinary actions of every day. We need not, then, seek for difficult works, laborious duties, multiplied spiritual exercises; we have in the daily duties, the means of attaining the highest sanctity. "Each action," to use the words of a devout author, "is all full of God, breathes of God, shines with God, is fragrant of God." . . .

. . . Our ordinary duties should be performed . . . "With all possible care and attention," none of which should be deemed trivial or unimportant. . . .

After all, what advantage are works to God? [It is] our working hearts He longs for. (*Familiar Instructions,* pp. 88–89)

Let us not feel distressed that others know our faults, for we all have our imperfections and will have them to our death. God [never bestows] all blessings on one person. He did not give to St. Peter what He gave to St. Paul nor to either what He gave to St. John. (*Retreat Instructions,* p. 182)

Reflection

The church's liturgical cycle, which embraces Advent, Christmas season, Lent, the Triduum, Easter season, and Ordinary Time, affirms that extraordinary moments themselves occur because people are faithful in ordinary moments. For example, we celebrate Christmas because Mary, in the way of ordinary pregnancies, carried Jesus daily for nine months.

Revelation or celebration emerges spontaneously when people appreciate the profound connection between ordinary and extraordinary experience, profane and sacred reality. Such appreciation allows us to realize that ordinary experience roots extraordinary experience in our humanity even as extraordinary experience stretches our humanity toward divinity. This ordinary experience creates the "stuff" of extraordinary experience even while celebration makes tolerable the dailiness of life.

Catherine McAuley understood the importance of this basic pattern in one's spirituality. She encouraged attention to the church's liturgical calendar as a way to focus the significance of each passing day. Because she also understood time as "the purchase money of eternity," she spoke strongly to the value of careful living, attentiveness to ordinary actions, as a way to prepare ourselves for celebration and revelation. "We are every day," she cautioned her young community, "preparing to enter our own country" (*Familiar Instructions*, p. 133). Every day and every ordinary action are opportunities to encounter and to love God and our sisters and brothers.

✦ Select an ordinary activity—dressing in the morning, preparing a meal, working on a project—and become aware of its many movements and details. What short, careful steps can you take toward making this activity an act of attention and love of God and your neighbor? Focus your attention on some of your daily activities with a short prayer like, "Each action, full of God."

✦ Review in your mind's eye the pattern of this past month. List the acts of self-denial and virtue that you observe in your experience. Was there an extraordinary moment? If so, how did this moment grow out of the ordinariness of life?

✦ Catherine tells us that the proof of love is deed. List a number of small ways you can demonstrate your love for someone close to you. Make a similar list of simple deeds by which you can reflect God's love for a neighbor or a coworker. Choose items from your list and put them into practice.

✦ Reflect on some of the liturgical readings from Ordinary Time. What do these readings teach us about the "dailiness" of Jesus? About being a Christian day to day?

✦ Create an extraordinary experience for someone.

God's Word

The truly capable woman—who can find her?
    She is far beyond the price of pearls.

. . . .

She selects wool and flax,
    she does her work with eager hands.

. . . .

She sets her mind on a field, then she buys it;
    with what her hands have earned she plants a
        vineyard.

She puts her back into her work
    and shows how strong her arms can be.

She knows that her affairs are going well;
    her lamp does not go out at night.

She sets her hands to the distaff,
    her fingers grasp the spindle.

She holds out her hands to the poor,
    she opens her arms to the needy.

Snow may come, she has no fears for her household,
    with all her servants warmly clothed.

She makes her own quilts,
    she is dressed in fine linen and purple.

. . . .

She is clothed in strength and dignity,
    she can laugh at the day to come.

When she opens her mouth, she does so wisely;
    on her tongue is kindly instruction.

She keeps good watch on the conduct of her household,
    no bread of idleness for her.

Her children stand up and proclaim her blessed,
    her husband, too, sings her praises:

"Many women have done admirable things,
    but you surpass them all!"

                            (Proverbs 31:10–29)

Closing prayer:

My God
I am Yours
for time and eternity.
Teach me to cast myself entirely
into the arms of
Your loving Providence
with the most lively, unlimited
confidence in Your
compassionate, tender pity.
Grant me,
O most merciful Redeemer,
that whatever
You ordain or permit
may be acceptable to me.
Take from my heart all painful anxiety;
suffer nothing to sadden me but sin,
nothing to delight me but the hope
of coming to the possession of You,
my God and my all,
in Your everlasting Kingdom.
Amen.

(Catherine McAuley)

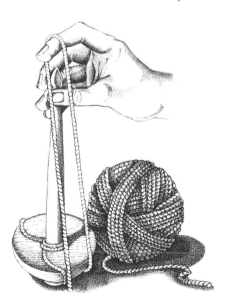

✦ Meditation 8 ✦

God's Comfort Comes

Theme: Catherine's conviction that "comfort comes soon after a well-received trial" enabled her to accept suffering with serenity (p. 118). Her experience taught her that God would soon come "both hands filled with favors and blessings" (*Letters*, p. 204).

Opening prayer: Constant God, be with me in the ebb and flow of life. Help me to know, in moments both of joy and of suffering, that your steadying, loving presence surrounds and sustains me.

About Catherine

Illness frequently visited Baggot Street. Hard work in difficult circumstances eventually took its toll on the community. In order to provide some respite and change of scenery for Sisters worn out and ill from their ministry, Catherine purchased a house in Kingstown, now the city of Dun Laughaire, on the seacoast north of Dublin. The Sisters assigned there would limit their ministry to the visitation of the sick poor. This attempt to provide some respite from trials ironically led to more trouble for Catherine.

Daily encounters with young girls loitering about Kingstown convinced the Sisters that a school was needed for them. Although she had no funds to undertake the project, Catherine offered the coach house, stables, and part of the garden for the ministry. The parish priest, Father Sheridan, agreed to help even though the parish was heavily in debt due to the construction of a new church. On the strength of this promise, Catherine proceeded with the necessary renovations.

With the work completed, the contractor sent the bill to Father Sheridan who then directed it to Baggot Street. Catherine and Father Sheridan each believed that the other should be responsible for the costs. Because she had offered the proceeds of the community's annual bazaar to start the work and had thus paid the contractor £50, Catherine was held responsible. The builder threatened to sue her.

Convinced that she had been wronged, Catherine decided to make her point by withdrawing the Sisters from Kingstown. Knowing that the poor girls would suffer from the closing of the project pained Catherine. In a letter to Teresa White, she said:

> I charge you, my very dear child, not to be sorrowful, but rather to rejoice if we are to suffer this humiliating trial. God will not be angry, be assured of that, and is not that enough? I feel that it would give you no consolation were I to say: "God would not be displeased with you, though He may be with me." He will not be displeased with me, for He knows I would rather be cold and hungry than the poor in Kingstown or elsewhere should be deprived of any consolation in our power to afford. But in the present case, we have done all that belonged to us to do, and even more than the circumstances justified. (*Letters,* pp. 142–143)

Shortly afterward Catherine wrote to Mary de Pazzi Delaney, "I cannot express the consolation Sister M. Teresa has afforded me by her manner of concluding the Kingstown business, and the few quiet lines she sent to Father Sheridan. Thanks be to God, I find the Sisters can act as well as could be desired when I am not at home" (*Letters,* p. 145).

Pause: Prepare a comfortable cup of tea and think of a story from your own life that reflects the interplay of joys and sorrow.

Catherine's Words

To Sr. M. Frances Warde, Catherine wrote:

> Thus we go on, my dear Sister Francis, flourishing in the very midst of the Cross, more than a common share of which has latterly fallen to my lot, thanks be to God. I humbly trust it is the Cross of Christ. I endeavor to make it, in some way like His, by silence. (P. 125)

> It distresses me very much to hear . . . that your good director was changed. I know it is an affliction to you, but rest assured, God will send some distinguished consolation. This is your life, joys and sorrows mingled, one succeeding the other. Let us not think of the means employed to convey to us a portion of the Holy Cross, being ever mindful that it came from Himself. You remember what Father Gaffney said to us when in Retreat: "If the entire Cross upon which Christ died was sent to the house, how impatient would each Sister be to carry it, and she who was permitted to keep it the longest would be the most favored. Far better and more profitable for you to receive with all your heart the Cross which God will send you in any form or shape He pleases." I earnestly hope that you will receive this trial so as to render it valuable to you. (*Letters*, p. 341)

Reflection

In all of the seasons of Catherine's life, joy and sorrow interplayed: the loss of the Callaghans gave her the means to begin her ministry; the community flourished despite the death of young Sisters; misunderstandings with some members of the clergy were balanced by the constant requests from bishops and priests for new foundations; the weariness and stress of continual travel were compensated for by the joy of seeing her Sisters and their efforts on behalf of the poor; distress at the need to correct a Sister became the occasion for playful verses in which the critique was softened.

The conviction that God would not leave her long in pain without some manifestation of love enabled Catherine to find peace in the midst of suffering. She urged this same serenity on the Sisters, reminding them that acceptance of sorrow as our portion of the cross of Christ increases the loving spirit within the community and engenders an atmosphere in which "there is no disunion, no gloomy depression of spirits, no departure from charity" (*Letters*, p. 115).

Catherine often declared her confidence in the steady and steadying love of God: "Some great thing which [God] designs to accomplish would have been too much without a little bitter in the cup. . . . He will soon come with both hands filled with favours and blessings" (*Letters*, p. 204).

✧ Read Ecclesiastes 3:1–11 and savor this scriptural description of the ebb and flow of life.

✧ Find a way to be a sign of God's blessing in the life of someone you know to be suffering.

✧ Search the daily paper for manifestations of God's caring presence in both the bad news and the good news.

✧ Catherine asks: If we take joy from the Lord, must we not also accept sorrow? How would the adoption of this attitude help to soften the transition between these experiences?

✧ List the major events of the past year. Find the rhythm of the joys and sorrows which succeeded one another during this time, in these events. Reflect on the richness of the pattern created in your life by the interweaving of these experiences.

✧ Pray the joyful and sorrowful mysteries of your own life. As you ponder joyful and sorrowful mysteries, end your reflection with Catherine's prayer: God will soon come with "both hands filled with favors and blessings."

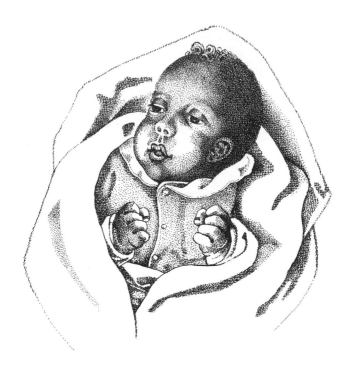

God's Word

"In all truth I tell you,
you will be weeping and wailing
while the world will rejoice;
you will be sorrowful,
but your sorrow will turn to joy.
A woman in childbirth suffers,
because her time has come;
but when she has given birth to the child she forgets the
    suffering
in her joy that a human being has been born into the
    world.
So it is with you: you are sad now,
but I shall see you again, and your hearts will be full of
    joy,
and that joy no one shall take from you."

(John 16:20–22)

Closing prayer:

My God,
I am Yours
for time and eternity.
Teach me to cast myself entirely
into the arms of
Your loving Providence
with the most lively, unlimited
confidence in Your
compassionate, tender pity.
Grant me,
O most merciful Redeemer,
that whatever
You ordain or permit
may be acceptable to me.
Take from my heart all painful anxiety;
suffer nothing to sadden me but sin,
nothing to delight me but the hope
of coming to the possession of You,
my God and my all,
in Your everlasting Kingdom.
Amen.

(Catherine McAuley)

Cordial Love, Something That Warms

Theme: Catherine believed that relationships based on cordial love and union of hearts lead us more deeply into the mystery of God's love and enable us to expend ourselves in service.

Opening prayer: Enveloping God, clothe me with love as with a garment. In all my actions and interactions may I put on Christ, wrapping myself in the mantle of mercy and justice. May all who encounter me, encounter your warming, nurturing love.

About Catherine

Warm love and playfulness marked relationships among the early women of Mercy. This spirit was evidenced in a series of letters surrounding the foundation of a Convent of Mercy in Birr. An exchange with Mary Ann Doyle, relating to overnight hospitality for the party traveling to Birr, was first in this series of warmhearted, good-humored, affectionate letters about the Sisters at Birr:

I wrote to Mother Mary Ann asking could she let five go to sleep on Saturday the 26th and could our devotions on

Sunday, breakfast and visit to the New Convent be over by 12 o'c. 2 post carriages ready to start for Birr. I prayed her to answer quickly, plainly, and briefly. She writes as follows: *Céad mille Failthe.* Good day's lodgings, entertainment for man and beast, coffee for teetotalers, Mass at 8 o'c. Breakfast 9:30, visit to New Convent at 10. 2 first-rate chaises from Head Inn at the door at 12. . . . Arrive in Birr at 4 o'c. No fog until 5. Dear Rev. Mother approach! (*Letters*, p. 274)

The fun-loving spirit with which Mary Ann Doyle warmed the travelers followed them into the town.

Although Catherine described the convent as a good house, the Sisters suffered from its damp coldness. Catherine joked about all of this in a steady stream of letters describing the first days of the new community. To two different Sisters, she said: "Here we are surrounded by Newfoundland Ice, obliged to keep hot turf under the butter to enable us to cut it" (p. 287); and "Sister A. M. laughs at the stirabout [oatmeal] that broke her tooth" (*Letters*, p. 293).

Even as she made light of it, Catherine suffered acutely from the cold: "All around me covered with snow, and my poor fingers petrified" (p. 297). And in another: "I feel the frost most acutely in my right side from my hip to my ankle. I have put on a great flannel bandage with camphorated spirit, and trust in God it will, like a dear good old acquaintance, carry me safe back" (*Letters*, p. 305).

While such conditions might be expected to dampen the spirits of the Sisters, Catherine proclaimed them invigorating:

> I have a little secret to tell you, don't proclaim it. I have my morning cloak on for a petticoat, the end of the sleeves sewed up, to make pockets. All my wardrobe is washing. I came home yesterday with at least half a yard of deep mud, melted snow. . . .
>
> Hurrah for foundations, makes the old young and the young merry. (*Letters*, p. 289)

A subsequent letter reports that the Sisters danced every evening: probably not only a sign of joyful spirits, but also an attempt to keep warm!

In the same letter in which she described the effect of the cold, she also wrote:

> On New Year's Day, after Mass, Dr. Spain said: "My dear people, I have a New Year's Gift for you, I have a present to make you, such as is most gratifying to a pastor's feelings. I present you the SISTERS OF MERCY, etc., etc." When we came home, Sister Anna Maria was most humorous. She said, quite in a whining melancholy voice: "He might have kept us a little longer, he need not have given us away so soon." She is all life and spirits. Nothing like foundations for bringing forth. (*Letters*, p. 289)

Pause: Prepare a comfortable cup of tea and think of a story from your own life when cordial love enabled a group to help one another through a difficult experience.

Catherine's Words

> Our charity is to be cordial. Now cordial signifies something that renews, invigorates, and warms. Such should be the effects of our love for each other. (Bolster, *Positio*, pp. 798–799)

> As it is impossible to love God without manifesting a love for our neighbor, so it is equally impossible to love our neighbor without exhibiting it to him in our conduct, for . . . we show our feelings by acts. . . . Banish from your heart all coldness, aversion, and reserve. . . We must have a warm, cordial affection for all and manifest it by words, action and manner. In fine, our charity must be in our hearts and from our hearts, and a charity such as Jesus Christ practiced while on earth. . . .
>
> Well-ordered charity begins at home. (*Retreat Instructions*, pp. 148, 153)

Reflection

In selecting locations for convents of Mercy, Catherine McAuley did not shrink from those that promised physical or ministerial challenges. At the same time, she knew that the demands of ministry and of community and the hardships encountered in many of her foundations could only be sustained through trust in God's providence, love, and support for one another, and playfulness and good humor. For instance, in the midst of the loneliness occasioned by the departure of a group of Sisters from Baggot Street, Catherine wrote, "Mother de Pazzi and I have kept up a regular concert of sighing and moaning since the Sisters went, but this day I was resolved not to be outdone, or even equalled, so commenced groaning for every sigh she gave, and our sorrows ended in laughing at each other" (*Letters*, p. 242). Many a harsh circumstance were softened in this way.

While she taught the Sisters to put their whole confidence in God who would never leave them in want, she also encouraged them to love one another warmly. She knew that such mutual, cordial love would sustain them in the difficulties that they faced. This cordial love manifested itself in a variety of forms: in particular gestures of kindness toward one another and in the teasing, dancing, and laughing that Catherine modeled and encouraged in community.

✧ Think of someone whose love "renews, invigorates, and warms" you. How do you experience these effects? Let the person know how her or his love enriches your life. Think of ways to extend that warming love to others.

✧ The cordial love with which Catherine animated her community was conveyed in her letters when she was not physically present. Begin a correspondence with someone whose circumstances would be lightened by this evidence of your love and concern.

✧ Catherine taught that "well-ordered charity begins at home." Is there someone in your family or neighborhood who needs the encouragement of some loving gesture? Ponder and pray about this, and then extend this well-ordered charity.

✧ Read the Gospel of Luke, with particular attention to the simple but very particular and personal gestures Jesus makes toward those he encounters in the Gospel stories. How can these kinds of interactions be incorporated into your relationships?

✧ Cultivate the practice of responding warmly to each person you meet throughout the day. To call yourself to such simple, cordial love, when you enter your workplace, your home, a meeting, or church—when you enter any place—pray these words: "God, may I remember that well-ordered charity begins at home."

✧ Think of the last time you were in a difficult situation with a group of people. What could you have done to lighten the situation? The next time you are in a similar circumstance, try to help the group move through it with humor and grace.

God's Word

My dear friends,
let us love each other,
since love is from God
and everyone who loves is a child of God and knows
    God.
Whoever fails to love does not know God,
because God is love.
This is the revelation of God's love for us,
that God sent [the] Son into the world
that we might have life through him.
Love consists in this:
it is not we who loved God,
but God loved us and sent [the] Son
to expiate our sins.
My dear friends,
if God loved us so much,
we too should love each other.
No one has ever seen God,
but as long as we love each other
God remains in us.

(1 John 4:7–13)

Closing prayer:

My God
I am Yours
for time and eternity.
Teach me to cast myself entirely
into the arms of
Your loving Providence
with the most lively, unlimited
confidence in Your
compassionate, tender pity.
Grant me,
O most merciful Redeemer,
that whatever
You ordain or permit
may be acceptable to me.
Take from my heart all painful anxiety;
suffer nothing to sadden me but sin,
nothing to delight me but the hope
of coming to the possession of You,
my God and my all,
in Your everlasting Kingdom.
Amen.

(Catherine McAuley)

✧ Meditation 10 ✧

Hospitality, Great Tenderness in All Things

Theme: Catherine's hospitality of heart offered welcome to strangers and a gracious countenance to familiar persons.

Opening prayer: Sheltering God, your mercy creates for all your creatures a place to be ourselves, to be healed toward wholeness. Free my heart to embrace those whom I do not know or do not love and to treat tenderly those whom I know and love.

About Catherine

Catherine's delightful sense of openness and welcome extended to herself as well as others. She often spoke with warmth and humor of her ailments, blunders, and administrative frustrations. She understood hospitality to be as much a matter of being at home with oneself as a matter of being at home with others.

Catherine's many years of caring for her sick mother and the Callaghans formed in her a special concern for the well-being of those women whose health was weak. She often insisted on special favors for the sick and the weary. A young woman whose health seemed a barrier to entering the congregation was given lodging in a convent near the sea. Catherine asked the sisters there if they could prepare a room for her and give her "all the care you can for a little while." They were also to embrace her weakened state with gentle concern. "Give her," Catherine writes, "a little broiled meat, or whatever she tells you she can take; [she's] not to get up until breakfast time, except you have Mass and she feels able. Not to go out except she likes to try a short walk. Great tenderness in all things" (*Correspondence*, p. 29).

Persons who were poor and burdened by life's worries received Catherine's special hospitality and warmth. "God knows," she once wrote, "that I would rather be cold and hungry, than the poor . . . should be deprived of any consolation in our power to afford [them]" (*Letters*, p. 142).

The gift of hospitality so prominent in Catherine's life marks the living memory of her death. The early community and all successive generations of Sisters of Mercy hold sacred a tradition stemming from her dying moments. In the few hours preceding her death, Catherine called each sister present at Baggot Street to her bedside. Each in her turn received a final word from the beloved founder. Then, turning to the infirmarian, Catherine said in a clear voice, "'Be sure you have a comfortable cup of tea for them when I am gone'" (Teresa Austin Carroll, *Life of Catherine McAuley*, p. 437). Catherine McAuley offered hospitality to the end.

Pause: Prepare a comfortable cup of tea and think of a story from your own life that reflects your understanding of hospitality.

Catherine's Words

Though a sister's state of health may prevent her from performing any of the active duties of the house or her incapacity to fill them may cause her to think she is of little or no value to the community, yet if she practices cordiality towards all her sisters she is doing a great deal both for God and for the community. She is then taking an active part in all the duties of the order. (*Retreat Instructions*, p. 62)

[Advice to a local superior] You must waste some time with visitors and introduce the Sisters. Make Sister M. T. come forward on all occasions while you are with her, that she may learn the manner of acting when you are not. (*Correspondence*, p. 170)

The prosperity or advancement of the order neither depends on nor should be attributed to the good reader, writer, or transcriber, although such are very desirable, but to the humble, cordial, affectionate, obliging, complying and charitable sister. (*Retreat Instructions*, p. 63)

Reflection

The derivation of the word *hospitality* itself connotes three distinct elements: house, guest, and host. The interplay of these three elements in the word's origin conveyed a sense of receiving the stranger as a welcome guest in one's home. Today the virtue might require Christian persons to understand themselves as guests in the home of Mother Earth; to welcome into the home of their hearts persons considered strange; to open the doors of nation and state to shelter those without home and family.

Hospitality has been trivialized in our culture. Product marketing promises warmth, concern, and friendship just to sell us things. Self-help, recreational, and interest-specific groups work hard to create a sense of belonging among persons whose human connectedness often remains rather shallow.

Like hosts who eat most of the food in front of the hungry guests, our society consumes an inequitable amount of the world's resources (food, oil, plants, and forests) without considering global needs or the well-being of other people. Persons considered different in cultural background, sexual orientation, skin color, or language skills often find themselves outside many circles of welcome and warmth.

On the other hand, being hospitable means being a good guest. By abusing the earth and the other inhabitants of the earth, we tear down the house that shelters us and wreck the table upon which we feast. Hospitable guests respect their hosts and do not abuse their welcome.

Catherine McAuley's world did not differ greatly from our own. She found ways to be courteous to poor people and her coworkers, and she encouraged simple living. She fostered a welcoming spirit within her works of mercy. In naming her first foundation the House of Mercy, she identified a fundamental value in her spirituality and in Christian living: hospitality. Indeed, all Christian homes should be houses of merciful hospitality.

✧ Write your reflections on the following questions: Where do you feel welcome? How does welcome feel? Where do you feel unwelcome? Why? How does unwelcome feel?

✧ Recall a time when you were a stranger and someone took you under their roof or wing. Offer a prayer of gratitude for their hospitality.

✧ Read carefully the story of the Shunemmite woman (2 Kings 4:8–11). What does that story tell us about the interchangeable nature of the roles of host and guest in Christian hospitality?

✧ Review the stories on the front page of today's newspaper. What do the stories tell us of the state of hospitality and common courtesy in the world today? How would an understanding of the world as "home for all" change the news you are reading?

✧ Practice hospitality. Invite someone who has never been a guest in your home to share a simple meal with you. Consider how you will prepare a welcome for this person as well as a meal.

✧ Offer a gesture of hospitality to the earth. Plant a tree; become involved in an organization with an earth-friendly focus; adopt an area in your neighborhood and keep it free of litter.

God's Word

Yahweh appeared to [Abraham] at the Oak of Mamre while he was sitting by the entrance of the tent during the hottest part of the day. He looked up, and there he saw three men standing near him. As soon as he saw them he ran from the entrance of the tent to greet them, and bowed to the ground. "My lord," he said, "If I find favour with you, please do not pass your servant by. Let me have a little water brought, and you can wash your feet and have a rest under the tree. Let me fetch a little bread and you can refresh yourselves before going further, now that you have come in your servant's direction." They replied, "Do as you say." (Genesis 18:1–5)

Closing prayer:

My God
I am Yours
for time and eternity.
Teach me to cast myself entirely
into the arms of
Your loving Providence
with the most lively, unlimited
confidence in Your
compassionate, tender pity.
Grant me,
O most merciful Redeemer,
that whatever
You ordain or permit
may be acceptable to me.
Take from my heart all painful anxiety;
suffer nothing to sadden me but sin,
nothing to delight me but the hope
of coming to the possession of You,
my God and my all,
in Your everlasting Kingdom.
Amen.

(Catherine McAuley)

✧ Meditation 11 ✧

I Leave You Free

Theme: Catherine strove to free people from what chained them, and to enable them to grow to the full flowering of their humanity.

Opening prayer: Empowering God, you fashioned the world and then entrusted it to humankind, confident that we would be good and faithful stewards of your creation. Help me to have the same confidence in those around me, calling forth their gifts and welcoming their collaboration in the work of building your Reign.

About Catherine

Catherine's enabling and ennobling spirit embraced the poor people that she loved and the women who joined her in their service. During her years at Coolock House, the idleness of the young women around the neighborhood concerned Catherine. She soon recognized that in addition to being unemployed, they had no transferable and marketable skills to use for employment. So Catherine began to teach them domestic skills and needlework. Eventually, she opened a shop as an outlet for the women's talents. The proceeds of the shop paid the artisans and enabled Catherine to expand the scope of her classes.

Catherine also encouraged the growth and autonomy of the women who joined her in the Community of Mercy. Because of the constant demands for new foundations, she often appointed young and inexperienced Sisters as superiors, trusting that challenging circumstances would draw out their fullest potential. She called upon the Sisters to use independent judgment in facing situations that confronted them.

When a Kingstown priest wrote to Catherine requesting the admission of a poor child to the Sisters' school, she promptly placed the matter in the hands of Teresa White, the local superior. Catherine expressed her opinion to Teresa, but made it clear that the decision was Teresa's to make:

> I do not think it would be well to have a child who could not remain always, but I leave you free to do what you think is best. I am satisfied that you will not act imprudently, and this conviction makes me happy. . . .
>
> I am not uneasy about the school business. You will do all you can. God help and preserve you, my dear child. (*Letters*, pp. 137, 139)

Catherine involved the Sisters in important decisions such as the selection of the Rule for the new community and the selection of Sisters who would go on foundations. Often, decisions flowed from conversations at evening recreation during which Catherine invited all to gather round her and discuss the decisions that needed to be made. Even members suffering from illness were empowered with a sense of contributing to the well-being of the community:

> Though a sister's state of health may prevent her from performing any of the active duties of the house or her incapacity to fill them may cause her to think she is of little or no value to the community, yet if she practices cordiality towards all her sisters she is doing a great deal both for God and for the community. She is then taking an active part in all the duties of the order. (*Retreat Instructions*, p. 62)

In an extraordinary gesture for her times, she made each foundation governmentally independent. She relied less on regulation than on the bonds of love to connect the Sisters to herself and to one another. These bonds were nurtured through regular visits and an outpouring of letters.

Her ultimate act of trust and gift of freedom came on the day of her death. Asked to name the Sister who would succeed her, Catherine replied, "The Constitutions give the Sisters the liberty of choosing for themselves, and I will not interfere by directing their choice" (*A Few of the Sayings, Instructions, and Prayers of the Foundress of the Sisters of Mercy,* p. 52).

Pause: Prepare a comfortable cup of tea and think of a story from your own life when someone's confidence in you enhanced your strength and creativity.

Catherine's Words

In Catherine McAuley's letters, she steadily encouraged the sisters to use their own abilities and powers:

> Every place has its own particular ideas and feelings which must be yielded to when possible. (P. 147)

> Never suppose you can make me feel displeasure by giving any opinion that occurs to you. (P. 165)

> Do not fear offending anyone. Speak as your mind directs and always act with . . . courage. (P. 353)

> Sister M. Aloysius perfectly at home, the most vigilant clever manager I have met in some time. I never knew till now the loss she must have been to her Father's large family. We put our candles under a bushel . . . I never cease thanking God for giving me courage to bring her into action and she is delighted. (Pp. 291, 293)

> I have found the second visit to a new branch exceedingly useful. Not for what we can say or do, for our experience in religious life has been so short that a good faithful Sister, to whom God has imparted grace may be said to know as much of spiritual life as we do, yet it is certainly most useful to give assistance for some time. It animates the new beginners, and gives confidence to others. (*Letters,* p. 331)

In the Rule, Catherine institutionalized the empowerment of women:

> No work of charity can be more productive of good to society, or more conducive to the happiness of the poor, than the careful instruction of women. (2:5)

Reflection

Love and respect for every person, taught to Catherine by the example of her father, flowered during her years with the Callaghans. Here Catherine not only received encouragement and financial support for her work among the poor but also, contemporary writers suggest, was significantly influenced by the attitudes and practices of the Society of Friends—Mrs. Callaghan's religion. George Fox, founder of the Society of Friends, believed that "'there is that of God in every man'" (Bourke, *A Woman Sings of Mercy*, p. 26). Catherine agreed.

Catherine's profound respect for the dignity of each person and her own experience of having had to be dependent on the goodness of others for her bread and board created in her an urgency not only to help the poor, but to impart the skills necessary for them to live independently, thus enabling them to achieve their full potential as daughters and sons of God.

The manner in which Catherine governed the Community of Mercy also clearly manifests the Quaker influence: "Particularly important in the shaping of Catherine McAuley was the Quaker respect and appreciation for the talents of women. Their pioneering acknowledgment of the spiritual equality of men and women liberated Quaker women to share both religious and secular responsibilities" (Regan and Keiss, *Tender Courage*, p. 16). Catherine exemplified this same belief in her genuine respect for the persons and talents of the sisters.

Indeed, fostering the good of other people and nurturing their powers and potential are fundamental to Christian love.

✧ One of the primary sources of powerlessness in our society is lack of reading skills. Enroll in a literacy program and empower others by teaching them to read.

✧ Resolve to find, each day, at least one way to praise and encourage someone with whom you live or work.

✧ Reflect on Luke 9:1–6, particularly on the manner in which Jesus empowers the Twelve Apostles.

✧ Reflect on the healing miracles of Jesus. Read and ponder your favorite story of healing. Ask yourself: What is the relationship between healing and empowerment for mission?

✧ Think of some latent talent or skill you have wanted to develop: for instance, learning a second language, playing an instrument, sewing, or cooking. Decide on a course of action and then do it!

God's Word

The seventy-two came back rejoicing. "Lord," they said, "even the devils submit to us when we use your name." He said to them, "I watched Satan fall like lightning from heaven. Look, I have given you power to tread down serpents and scorpions and the whole strength of the enemy; nothing shall ever hurt you. Yet do not rejoice that the spirits submit to you; rejoice instead that your names are written in heaven." (Luke 10:17–20)

Closing prayer:
My God,
I am Yours
for time and eternity.
Teach me to cast myself entirely
into the arms of
Your loving Providence
with the most lively, unlimited
confidence in Your
compassionate, tender pity.
Grant me,
O most merciful Redeemer,
that whatever

You ordain or permit
may be acceptable to me.
Take from my heart all painful anxiety;
suffer nothing to sadden me but sin,
nothing to delight me but the hope
of coming to the possession of You,
my God and my all,
in Your everlasting Kingdom.
Amen.

(Catherine McAuley)

✧ Meditation 12 ✧

Equal Reason to Rejoice

Theme: Catherine was convinced that all things worked toward good for those who loved God, self, and others. From that deep appreciation of life flowed a light, whimsical sense of humor.

Opening prayer: Laughing God, startle me into an appreciation for the delightful incongruity of life. Teach my heart to hear laughter echo in all your creation. Help me to enjoy the gift of humor in myself and others.

About Catherine

During the last five years of Catherine's life, a chronic cough signaled the disease that would take her life. Arthritic pain and stiffness, broken limbs, and strained muscles plagued her. In addition, revenues from the annual bazaar were seriously reduced, and a possible lawsuit threatened the community's meager financial resources. Challenging personalities within her growing congregation created tensions and, in some instances, controversy. Death continued to claim friends, relatives, and Sisters of Mercy with alarming frequency.

Even so, Catherine kept her keen sense of humor. Only a person centered in the richness of God's mercy and goodness could find reason, in the midst of these trials and frustrations, for the lighthearted banter and whimsical verse found in her correspondence. Catherine McAuley's humor was gentle and loving. She knew how to laugh at herself and to laugh with others. No one was spared her wit and no moment was considered too solemn for its exercise.

The first English Sister of Mercy, Lady Barbara Eyre, discovered early in her journey in Mercy the founder's love for practical jokes. Lady Eyre's family was highly connected in English society. Prior to her reception into the Order of Mercy, a note from Her Majesty's hairdresser arrived at the Bermondsey convent: "'By desire of the Countess Constantia Clifford, Monsieur Trufitt will wait on the Sisters of Mercy at nine o'clock on Thursday morning to adjust a court headdress'" (Degnan, *Mercy Unto Thousands*, p. 254).

Early on the day of the ceremony, Catherine went to Lady Barbara's room, disguised her voice, and said, "Please, your Ladyship, Monsieur Trufitt is come." Lady Barbara, having her back to Catherine and unaware of the deception, replied, "'Take down that box with my feathers and diamonds'" (Degnan, *Mercy Unto Thousands*, p. 254). Only when she turned around did she realize to her embarrassment and chagrin that the visitor was Reverend Mother rather than her hairdresser.

When Bishop John England came to Baggot Street to seek Sisters for Charleston, South Carolina, Catherine faced the situation with her own form of wit. The Baggot Street foundation had been depleted of sisters by previous generosity. At this particular time, only two novices, two sisters visiting from another convent, and the staff of the House of Mercy itself resided in the house.

After breakfast the women assembled in the community room from all quarters—laundry, dining room, and so on. Bishop England asked: "Who will come to Charleston with me to act as Superior?" According to Catherine's plan and amidst much laughter, the youngest postulant came forward. "'I had arranged it with her before,'" wrote Catherine, "'but did not think she would have the courage'" (Degnan, *Mercy Unto Thousands*, p. 318).

When the joke was on her, Catherine was equally pleased to encourage merriment. In a letter to Sr. M. Frances Warde, she described a visit to the Presentation Convent where she had made her novitiate:

We visited our old George's Hill—they were delighted, and so was I—said I would kiss the chairs and tables, but by some mistake I kissed a grand new chair in the parlor; however . . . I took it back and brought it up to the old rush chair I used to sit on in the noviceship. (*Letters*, p. 177)

Catherine's letters are filled with limericks written for her own amusement and that of her companions. Records also indicate that she would enter heartily into the simple entertainments of feast days and holidays, often performing to the delight of all. "Be cheerful," she counseled, "animating all around you" (*Letters*, p. 118).

Pause: Prepare a comfortable cup of tea and think of the times when humor has literally "saved the day" or saved a particular situation.

Catherine's Words

A fine example of Catherine's humor comes to us in a letter she wrote to a novice in the Tullamore convent in anticipation of a visit she would be making there. In the midst of the playfulness of her exchange, Catherine manages to convey some lessons for life and spiritual growth:

I really long for the time we are to meet again, please God. But the good Mother Superior will not have equal reason to rejoice, for I am determined not to behave well, and you must join me. If I write to mention the day we propose going, you might contrive to put the clock out of order, though that would be almost a pity. By some means we must have till ten o'clock every night, not a moment's silence until we are asleep—not to be disturbed until we awake. Take care to have the key of the [chapel], and when those who are not so happily disposed, go into the choir, we can lock them in until after breakfast. . . .

I know very well Father Murtagh will applaud our pious intention, for such it really is, when rightly considered. First, it will effectually remove all the painful remembrance of our former separation and animate us to go through a second parting. It will show superiors and their assistants that it is necessary sometimes to yield to the inclinations of others, and convince them that authority, however good, cannot always last. It also affords them an opportunity, if they will take advantage of it, of seeing dispositions and manners, that might remain unknown to them, and consequently unchanged. . . .

We will set up for a week what is called a Nonsensical Club. I will be President, you Vice-President, and Catherine can give lectures as Professor of Folly. (*Letters*, pp. 78–79)

Reflection

John S. Mogabgab, editor of *Weavings*, provides this perspective on humor:

Humor is but one sign of a more encompassing spiritual posture. Paul calls it *hilarotes*, "cheerfulness" (Romans 12:8). This is neither a superficial cheeriness that twitters along in determined denial of cloudy days, nor the "boisterous conviviality" suggested by contemporary connotations of the English word "hilarity." Rather, *hilarotes* has more to do with an ever-widening appreciation for God's gifts as the cornerstone of human life. ("Editor's Introduction," vol. 9, November–December 1994, pp. 2–3)

Christian humor comes from a free and trusting spirit secure in its confidence in God's love and the goodness of God's creation.

The word *humor* derives from a Latin word that means to be wet or moist. *Wit* has its origins in words meaning wisdom or knowledge. Both words help us understand the roles of humor and wit. Humor, like rain, helps us grow past the dry times. When life seems desperate, wit can invite us back to the wisdom that God loves us and guides life. Because Christ has saved us, we can rejoice. This wit—wisdom and knowledge—can help us laugh in the face of trials.

This is the humor reflected in the life of Catherine McAuley and is most appropriate for every Christian life. The place of such God-centered joy among the gifts of the Spirit has too often been lost in contemporary books on spirituality and prayer. As a result we often miss the humor in the sacred Scriptures and in the revelations of daily life. "If God is for us, who can be against us?" (Romans 8:31). Therefore, let us rejoice and be glad.

✧ Reflect on the manner in which humor brightens your day. How would you describe the characteristics of the person whose humor you most enjoy? What do you learn about this person's spiritual gifts through the lens of his or her humor?

✧ Read carefully one of the Gospel narratives with an eye to the humor present in God's word and God's world, the instances of incongruity and playfulness. Peter provides some of the best humor. See Matthew 14:22–33 and 16:22–23 for examples.

✧ Ponder a dilemma facing you, an unpleasant situation that bothers you. Pray for the grace to bring humor to the situation and to have the wit—wisdom—to rejoice and be glad in the midst of it. And remember, science teaches us that humor is good for our physical and mental well-being. Laughter aids digestion, reduces stress, and releases creativity.

✧ Write a limerick that will bring a moment of humor to the lives of friends or colleagues. Remember that a limerick is exclusively humorous and nonsensical; lines 1, 2, and 5 have three anapestic feet and rhyme with each other; lines 3 and 4 have two anapestic feet and rhyme with each other. Here is a sample:

> Some folly did Kitty desire
> Which the bending of rules did require.
> Said she of the gloomy,
> "Just bring the key to me,
> And we'll lock them all safe in the choir!"

✧ Find a book of humorous writings such as Phyllis McGinley's poetry or Erma Bombeck's essays. Watch a light-hearted video of your favorite comic actors. Enjoy their gift of humor and be grateful for their talent.

God's Word

He entered Jericho and was going through the town and suddenly a man whose name was Zacchaeus made his appearance; he was one of the senior tax collectors and a wealthy man. He kept trying to see which Jesus was, but he was too short and could not see him for the crowd; so he ran ahead and climbed a sycamore tree to catch a glimpse of Jesus who was to pass that way. When Jesus reached the spot he looked up and spoke to him, "Zacchaeus, come down. Hurry, because I am to stay at your house today." And he hurried down and welcomed him joyfully. (Luke 19:1–6)

Closing prayer:

My God,
I am Yours
for time and eternity.
Teach me to cast myself entirely
into the arms of
Your loving Providence
with the most lively, unlimited
confidence in Your
compassionate, tender pity.
Grant me,
O most merciful Redeemer,
that whatever
You ordain or permit
may be acceptable to me.
Take from my heart all painful anxiety;
suffer nothing to sadden me but sin,
nothing to delight me but the hope
of coming to the possession of You,
my God and my all,
in Your everlasting Kingdom.
Amen.

(Catherine McAuley)

✧ **Meditation 13** ✧

Waiting on God's Will

Theme: Catherine learned that hopeful expectation is the stance of one who trusts in the rhythm of God's own time.

Opening prayer: Eternal God, all the days of my life are in your hands. Help me to know your presence in each unfolding event; your active, enabling grace in every circumstance.

About Catherine

Catherine lived for twenty years with William and Catherine Callaghan. During that time, her responsibilities multiplied as did her involvement with charities. As the Callaghans aged, more and more of the management of Coolock House and the administration of the surrounding estate fell to her.

These were not empty years. Overseeing the Callaghan estate afforded Catherine experience in business and management. As the Callaghans' age led to infirmity, she offered care and companionship to her adoptive parents. Reading to Mrs. Callaghan during her illness steeped her in the Scriptures to an extent unusual for Catholics of her day. Provided with funds the Callaghans had earmarked for charitable causes, she ministered to the poor of Coolock village.

Desirous of support for her own faith journey, she gathered Catholic children and household servants for prayer and religious instruction. Instructing the children and caring for the needs of the poor sharpened her sense of ministry. When the Callaghan fortune became available to her, Catherine was poised to respond with wisdom and focus to the opportunities presented by her inheritance. Attentiveness to the experience and meaning of each day as it unfolded invested these years of waiting with a dynamic quality.

Catherine was twenty years old when her mother died; twenty-five when she went to live with the Callaghans; forty-four when she inherited Coolock House, and forty-nine when she built the House of Mercy on Baggot Street. For all those forty-nine years she waited for God's plan to become manifest in her life. During all those years of active and expectant waiting, she was being prepared for her future ministries as educator, social worker, home health nurse, and spiritual guide. Catherine McAuley knew that God required her "to make some lasting efforts for the relief of the suffering and instruction of the ignorant" (Bolster, *In Her Own Words*, p. 31).

Pause: Prepare a comfortable cup of tea and think of a story from your own life that reflects waiting for God.

Catherine's Words

On hearing that a young Sister had died, Catherine wrote to Sister Elizabeth:

> No words could describe what I felt on reading the first line of your letter. . . .
>
> God will support you in this great affliction. His Holy Will be done. . . . Some grand motive must actuate all His visitations.
>
> I will be in great anxiety to hear though I will be agitated at the sight of your next letter. May God bless and preserve you and grant you all humble, cheerful submission to the Divine Will. (*Letters*, pp. 203–204)

When Catherine had read Sister Elizabeth's next letter, she responded:

> I have cried heartily and implored God to comfort you. I know He will. . . . Some joyful circumstance will soon prove that God is watching over your concerns, which are all His own, but without the Cross the real Crown cannot come. Some great thing which He designs to accomplish would have been too much without a little bitter in the cup. (*Letters*, p. 204)

Catherine often had to take her own advice to patiently wait for God's will to be known. She wrote Sr. M. Frances Warde:

> These good Bishops take their own full time to consider any little affair, and those that are, like myself rather impatient for an answer, may just as well make up the mind to wait for one. (*Letters*, p. 363)

Reflection

In John's Gospel we meet Jesus who is conscious that time is in God's hands. At Cana, Jesus declares, "'My hour has not yet come'" (John 2:5). In the Priestly prayer, he says, "'Father, the hour has come: glorify your Son so that your Son may glorify you'" (John 17:1). Jesus is conscious not only that the unfolding of his life is in God's hands, but that God's purposes are fulfilled in God's own time.

Catherine McAuley had this same trust that God's will would be manifest when God wished and that the timing would be right. So even though she suffered from impatience at times, in the larger picture she knew that God's will would be known and that God's grace would be sufficient for her to do it.

✦ Reflect on the experiences of waiting in your own life. Ponder the difference between empty waiting and waiting that is expectant.

❖ Remember a time in your life when you waited for God. What gifts came to you during that time? Remember a time when you were conscious of asking God to wait for you. What did you come to understand in this experience? What did you learn about God's rhythm, your rhythm at these times?

❖ Visit someone whose life is clearly focused on waiting—expectant parents, an elderly person, a person with a terminal illness. Ask for a share of the wisdom engendered by this life experience.

❖ In a culture demanding instant gratification, waiting is becoming a lost art. Visualize yourself in a circumstance in which you may have to wait: for a bus, to see a doctor, in a traffic jam. What can you do to render this waiting time more creative and fruitful?

❖ Seek out someone for whom time is burdensome, perhaps a prisoner or a shut-in. Find a way to help relieve that burden.

❖ If you have been waiting to know God's will in some matter, pray to know God's will, for patience in waiting until you do, and the grace to respond once God's will is clearer.

God's Word

Be patient until Christ comes again. Ponder the patience of farmers who wait for the fruit to ripen in the sun and rain. You also need to be patient. Don't become distressed because Christ will come soon. Stop complaining about one another, so that you will not be judged yourself. Remember that the divine Judge waits. Look to the prophets as your models of patience in the midst of persecution. Perseverance in righteousness brings with it the title Blessed. (Adapted from James 5:7–11)

Closing prayer:

My God,
I am Yours
for time and eternity.
Teach me to cast myself entirely
into the arms of
Your loving Providence
with the most lively, unlimited
confidence in Your
compassionate, tender pity.
Grant me,
O most merciful Redeemer,
that whatever
You ordain or permit
may be acceptable to me.
Take from my heart all painful anxiety;
suffer nothing to sadden me but sin,
nothing to delight me but the hope
of coming to the possession of You,
my God and my all,
in Your everlasting Kingdom.
Amen.

(Catherine McAuley)

✧ Meditation 14 ✧

Entering the Spirit of the Church

Theme: Catherine's life reflects her understanding of the church as a community of believers joined in ritual, belief, and service.

Opening prayer: Gathering God, move me to look beyond ecclesial limitations of structure, person, and insight to gifts of tradition, holiness, and revelation. Deepen in me an appreciation for the powerful witness of an ecclesial community whose historical presence shows forth the wonder of God-with-us generation after generation.

About Catherine

As a bright young woman Catherine was often chagrined and embarrassed in conversations with her Protestant friends and relatives. She was little prepared to defend or explain the faith she held so dearly. As soon as she was free to do so, she studied the tenets of Catholicism in order to deepen her own faith and to share the beauty of its Tradition with others. These early struggles gave her a special regard for the instruction of the faithful in whose lives she understood the church to be revealed.

Toward the end of her life, she collaborated with Mary Vincent Deasy to write a quaint little book for such instructional purposes. Mary Vincent, working among poor people in Cork, remembered a story Catherine had probably related during their days together at Baggot Street. She asked the founder if she would record the tale to serve as a tool for her work instructing the people of Cork. Catherine sent the manuscript in February 1838, and Mary Vincent immediately set about editing the work for publication.

The resulting pamphlet, *Cottage Controversy,* clearly reveals Catherine's appreciation of a church living in the faith, practices, and witness of its people. The founder herself, in a letter of introduction, refers to the work as a useful tract for the instruction of converts "who require something amusing as well as instructive" (p. 3). Through a hundred-and-some pages of dialog, Margaret Lewis instructs Lady P— in the essential beliefs of Roman Catholicism. Witty and engaging conversation flows through a homey narrative sensitive to the rhythm of ordinary life.

Although Father Peter, "a curate . . . who concealed great learning and resolution under a simple exterior" (p. 7), is introduced early in the small work, Margaret Lewis, "a humble cottager" (p. 5), is the teacher and spokesperson for the church. Through a series of six conversations in the living room of her cottage, Margaret carefully instructs her benefactor, Lady P—, in the doctrines of the Catholic faith. Interspersed with these discussions of doctrine are vignettes that speak to the charity, devotional practices, and lively faith of the Lewis family.

In the second conversation, an exchange takes place that may well summarize Catherine's own understanding of the nature of the church:

Lady [P—]. But why do you believe all this? Is it merely because the priest tells it to you?

Margaret. It is because the whole Catholic Church teaches it, my lady, and a good reason it is if you would only think of it. For who would imagine that God would suffer such thousands and millions of holy and learned people as have lived and died in this faith . . . to remain in error? (Pp. 32–33)

In another passage Margaret speaks of the "learned and ignorant, wise and simple, poor and rich, priest and people" in whom the same faith in Christ is found and through whom Christ's word is preached (p. 29).

Cottage Controversy does not end in the conversion of Lady P—. Rather the work ends in mutual respect between the two women that allows a space for the faith of each.

Pause: Prepare a comfortable cup of tea and think of a story from your own life that best summarizes your relationship with the church.

Catherine's Words

How rapidly the days, weeks, and months are passing. Another month ended, that seemed but a few days begun. If we have not forfeited the friendship of almighty God, but have been trying to love Him more and more, and to serve Him faithfully, then they were blessed days for us. Oh, let us endeavour to use these days [Lent], such as we should wish the past to have been. Let us enter into the spirit of the Church . . . performing all with humble heart. (*Letters*, p. 310)

We may perceive from all our instructions that a strong and lively faith is the solid foundation of all virtue. (*Familiar Instructions*, p. 134)

Try to act so at all times, and in all places, that if our Divine Lord were to appear on earth again, He might not be ashamed to point you out, as one intimately united with Him, and nearly allied to Him. (Sisters of Mercy, *Thoughts from the Spiritual Conferences of Mother M. Catherine McAuley*, pp. 17–18)

Reflection

Catherine keenly remembered the house church presided over by her father. James McAuley consciously claimed his baptismal responsibility to teach, serve, and praise God within his family and his neighborhood. From early childhood, Catherine understood the importance of doctrine, service, and worship. Church embraced all aspects of one's existence.

Catherine was well into her mid-twenties before she was able to regularly attend church liturgies presided over by a clergyman. While she deeply appreciated this institutional aspect of the church, she focused her attention on the people whose daily witness proclaimed the mystery of the public institution.

Biographer Angela Bolster remarked that "the main arteries of Catherine McAuley's spirituality were the traditional Church devotions [of her time] which she embodied in her Holy Rule . . . the Sacred Heart, the Eucharist, the Passion, and the Blessed Virgin Mary under 'her sweet title of Mercy'" (*Positio*, p. 798). Her letters include frequent references to important feasts and seasons of the church year from which she drew inspiration and blessing. The rhythms of the church year offered Catherine and all the faithful an opportunity to be continually renewed in their intent to become Christ present to Christ's people.

Catherine had no desire to be an anonymous Catholic nor did she feel a need to constantly proselytize. She felt only a need to be faithfully, steadily, and overtly the baptized person she was.

✦ Examine your relationship with the church. What roles does it play in your spirituality? What images, events, or people of the church have you found inspiring? How has the church deepened your ability to love God and your neighbor? What do you find troublesome about the church? What commitment to the church do you want for yourself right now?

✦ In whatever liturgical season you find yourself today, "enter into the spirit of the Church" by reflecting on the meaning of this particular season and the richness it brings to your life.

✦ Catherine McAuley encouraged her Sisters to enrich their spiritual lives through devotion to the Sacred Heart, the

Passion, the Eucharist, and Mary, the mother of Jesus. Ponder this question: How could I create contemporary expressions of these devotions that reflect their deepest meaning and strengthen my faith? Dialog with Christ or a friend about this question.

✧ Membership in the church is reflected in belief, worship, and service. Define and implement ways to strengthen each of these dimensions of your life as a member of the church.

God's Word

These remained faithful to the teaching of the apostles, [and to the communal life,] to the breaking of bread and to the prayers.

And everyone was filled with awe; the apostles worked many signs and miracles.

And all who shared the faith owned everything in common; they sold their goods and possessions and distributed the proceeds among themselves according to what each one needed.

Each day, with one heart, they regularly went to the Temple but met in their houses for the breaking of bread; they shared their food gladly and generously; they praised God and were looked up to by everyone. Day by day the Lord added to their community those destined to be saved. (Acts 2:42–47)

Closing prayer:
My God
I am Yours
for time and eternity.
Teach me to cast myself entirely
into the arms of
Your loving Providence
with the most lively, unlimited
confidence in Your
compassionate, tender pity.

Grant me,
O most merciful Redeemer,
that whatever
You ordain or permit
may be acceptable to me.
Take from my heart all painful anxiety;
suffer nothing to sadden me but sin,
nothing to delight me but the hope
of coming to the possession of You,
my God and my all,
in Your everlasting Kingdom.
Amen.

(Catherine McAuley)

A Step Toward Eternity

Theme: In the course of her life, Catherine grew from fearing death to welcoming this movement of the human spirit to "that heavenly country" whose wonders we daily seek.

Opening prayer: Living God, in whose life we live and move and have our being, open my heart to the great mystery of passage from this life to the next life. Help me understand that in living well I die, and in dying well I live.

About Catherine

Catherine spent much of her life keeping vigil at the bedside of the dying. Many of these persons were close relatives or young women who belonged to the new sisterhood of Mercy. The earliest experience of such a vigil left Catherine with deep anxiety and fear of her own dying. As a twenty-year-old woman, Catherine nursed her mother, Elinor, through a long and painful illness and her eventual death.

Much of the pain of Elinor's dying arose from a struggle of conscience. She was born Catholic, raised Catholic, and had seen to the same for her children. With the clarity of approaching death, however, Elinor realized she had sacrificed much of the vitality of her Catholicism in favor of social pursuits and an inoffensive presence among her Protestant relatives and friends. She wished to be taken seriously as a social peer and could not afford, therefore, to take too seriously her faith, which was ridiculed in these same circles.

On her deathbed, she regretted her choice, but felt unsure that God's mercy could forgive such a lukewarm faith. By the time Elinor concluded that forgiveness was possible, she was very close to her final hour. The priest who came to administer the sacraments to the dying woman had to move quickly through the prescribed rituals. The gracious and beautiful Elinor McAuley died an uneasy death within minutes of his concluding prayers. The scene left a lasting and disturbing impression on Catherine who was unable to speak of it, even years later.

Gifted as she was in comforting others in their dying, Catherine approached her own death with apprehension. However, her consistent journey with others toward their entrance into what Catherine termed "that heavenly country" seems gradually to have brought peace to her own spirit (*Retreat Instructions*, p. 185). In October 1838, she wrote to Mary Teresa White that there was across from her room "a most simple inviting tomb" that, along with its "large weeping ash," pleases the eye and "excites meditation of the most consoling kind" (*Letters*, p. 137).

That her choice of words in this letter reflects a gradual reconciliation with the phenomenon of death is apparent from Elizabeth Moore's description of Catherine's own dying in 1841:

> Of our dear Reverend Mother . . . what can I say but that she died the death of the just. . . . She told Sr. Genevieve . . . that she felt exceedingly happy. . . . When we thought her senses might be going and that it might be well to rouse attention by praying a little louder, she said, "No occasion, my darling, to speak so loud, I hear distinctly." . . . Ten minutes before eight o'clock . . . she calmly breathed her last sigh. I did not think it possible for human nature to have such self-possession at the awful moment of death, but she had an extraordinary mind in life and death. (Savage, *Catherine McAuley*, pp. 376, 378–379)

Pause: Prepare a comfortable cup of tea and consider your own feelings toward death.

Catherine's Words

"Each day is a step we make towards eternity, and we shall continue thus to step from day to day until we take the last step, which will bring us into the presence of God." (Bolster, *Venerable for Mercy,* p. 87)

We cannot afford to lose any more time. What remains is too short to prepare for that heavenly country to which we are journeying. (*Retreat Instructions,* p. 185)

[In caring for the sick,] where there is no hope of recovery, charity requires that we make it known gradually and cautiously, lest the patient be too much alarmed. We may suggest many motives for resignation; such as . . . the necessity that all lie under of leaving [the world], sooner or later; the happiness of dying in God's grace . . . the joys of Heaven; the peace experienced by those who are entirely conformed to the will of God. (*Familiar Instructions,* p. 21)

Reflection

A variety of euphemisms for death allow us to hold extensive conversations without ever mentioning the simple words "death," "dying," or "dead." Technology promises an impressive array of solutions to the deterioration of our body. Psychology and new age spirituality offer myriad ways to strengthen mind and spirit against vulnerability and diminishment.

While much good has derived from technology, psychology, and the rediscovery of spirituality, we still die. Denying death helps none of us. This world is transitory, at best. If we do not face this fact, we fail to prepare ourself for the fullness of our humanity.

Illness and dying are a part of life. Physician Rachel Naomi Remen asserts that full living means "to grow in wisdom and to learn to love better. If life serves these purposes, then health serves these purposes and illness serves them as well" ("Spirit: Resource for Healing," *Noetic Sciences Review*, no. 27, Autumn 1993, p. 62). Dying and death understood in this manner become, as Catherine learned so well in her lifetime, a gateway to richer purpose, to deeper wisdom and love.

✧ Visit with someone who knows they are dying. If they are willing, share with them your feelings regarding death and ask them to share theirs with you. If you both feel comfortable, pray together for whatever kind of healing you need most.

✧ As a way of interacting with the reality of your own death and as an act of kindness to your family, make necessary decisions about your death and dying: enact advance directives for your health care; make arrangements for your funeral; write your obituary; plan your funeral services in a way that reflects your values and beliefs about your life here and hereafter.

✧ Imagine people gathered for your funeral. What would you want them to remember about you? To forget? What story would you want them to tell about you?

✧ Reread the story of the raising of Lazarus (John 11:1–44). Write a continuation of the story in which Lazarus describes to Mary and Martha his experiences during his four days in the tomb.

✧ Make time to be present to someone who is grieving.

✧ Select a favorite tree in your neighborhood. Watch it as it passes through the seasonal cycle of death and rebirth. What lessons does this tree hold for your own journey to that heavenly country?

God's Word

Suddenly I saw a new heaven and new earth. . . . I saw
the new Jerusalem, the holy city emerging out of heaven
from the hand of God, just like a bride who has dressed
for her husband. . . . Then a loud voice called from the
throne, "God lives here among human beings. God will
dwell among them. They will be God's people. They will
have no other God, but God-with-them. God will cleanse
their cheeks of tears, and death will cease as will grieving,
suffering, and sadness. Gone is the old world. (Adapted
from Revelation 21:1–4)

Closing prayer:

My God,
I am Yours
for time and eternity.
Teach me to cast myself entirely
into the arms of
Your loving Providence
with the most lively, unlimited
confidence in Your
compassionate, tender pity.
Grant me,
O most merciful Redeemer,
that whatever
You ordain or permit
may be acceptable to me.
Take from my heart all painful anxiety;
suffer nothing to sadden me but sin,
nothing to delight me but the hope
of coming to the possession of You,
my God and my all,
in Your everlasting Kingdom.
Amen.

(Catherine McAuley)

M·E·R·C·Y

✧ For Further Reading ✧

Bolster, M. Angela. *Catherine McAuley in Her Own Words.* Dublin, Ireland: Diocesan Office for Causes, 1978.

———. *Catherine McAuley: Venerable for Mercy.* Dublin, Ireland: Dominican Publications, 1990.

———. *The Correspondence of Catherine McAuley, 1827–1841.* Dioceses of Cork and Ross, Ireland: The Congregation of the Sisters of Mercy, 1989.

Bourke, M. Carmel. *A Woman Sings of Mercy: Reflections on the Life and Spirit of Mother Catherine McAuley, Foundress of the Sisters of Mercy.* Alexandria, Australia: E. J. Dwyer, 1987.

Degnan, M. Bertrand. *Mercy Unto Thousands: Life of Mother Mary Catherine McAuley, Foundress of the Sisters of Mercy.* Westminster, MD: The Newman Press, 1957.

Neumann, M. Ignatia, ed. *Letters of Catherine McAuley.* Baltimore: Helicon Press, 1969.

Regan, M. Joanna, and Isabelle Keiss. *Tender Courage: A Reflection on the Life and Spirit of Catherine McAuley, First Sister of Mercy.* Chicago: Franciscan Herald Press, 1988.

Savage, Roland Burke. *Catherine McAuley: The First Sister of Mercy.* Dublin, Ireland: M. H. Gill and Son, 1950.

Recordings

If you enjoy music, the following tapes provide another way of experiencing Catherine's spirit:

Circle of Mercy. Sisters of Mercy, 29000 Eleven Mile Road, Farmington Hills, MI 48336, USA.

Maxims of Catherine McAuley. C/o Cynthia Serjak, RSM, Convent of Mercy, 3333 Fifth Avenue, Pittsburgh, PA 15213, USA.

Acknowledgments *(continued)*

The excerpts on pages 14 (first excerpt), 24 (second excerpt), and 104 (first excerpt) are from *Catherine McAuley in Her Own Words*, by M. Angela Bolster (Dublin, Ireland: Diocesan Office for Causes, 1978), pages 31, 34, and 31, respectively. Copyright © 1978 by M. Angela Bolster.

The excerpts on pages 14 (second excerpt), 28 (second excerpt), and 115 (third excerpt) are from *Catherine McAuley: The First Sister of Mercy*, by Roland Burke Savage (Dublin, Ireland: M. H. Gill and Son, 1950), pages 393; 376; and 376 and 378–379, respectively.

The excerpts on pages 15, 16, 29–30, 30 (first and second excerpts), 36 (first excerpt), 36 (third excerpt), 42 (third excerpt), 50, 80 (second excerpt), and 111 are from *Prot. N. 1296: Dublin Documentary Study: Catherine McAuley*, vol. 1 (Rome, 1985), pages 841, 66, 830–831, 782, 817, 817, 775–776, 818, 798–799, and 798, respectively. Copyright © 1985 by M. Angela Bolster. Used with permission of the Sisters of Mercy, Dublin, Ireland.

The excerpts on pages 17, 20 (second excerpt), 34, and 93 (third excerpt) are from *Tender Courage: A Reflection on the Life and Spirit of Catherine, First Sister of Mercy*, by M. Joanna Regan and Isabelle Keiss (Chicago: Franciscan Herald Press, 1988), pages 14, 16, 46, and 16, respectively. Copyright © 1988 by Franciscan Herald Press. Used with permission.

The excerpts on pages 20 (first excerpt), 36 (second excerpt), 46 (third excerpt), 56 (first excerpt), 57, and 93 (second excerpt) are from *A Woman Sings of Mercy: Reflections on the Life and Spirit of Mother Catherine McAuley, Foundress of the Sisters of Mercy*, by M. Carmel Bourke (Alexandria, Australia: E. J. Dwyer, Unit 13 Perry Park, 33 Maddox Street, Alexandria NSW 2015, 1987), pages 4, 48, 71–72, 8, 79, and 26, respectively. Copyright © 1987 by M. Carmel Bourke. Used with permission of the publisher.

The excerpts on pages 22–23, 26, 27, 28 (first excerpt), 29 (first excerpt), 31 (third and fourth excerpts), 31 (sixth excerpt), 35 (first and second excerpts), 35 (third excerpt), 35 (fourth excerpt), 41 (sixth excerpt), 42 (first excerpt), 46 (first excerpt), 46 (second excerpt), 46–47, 51 (third excerpt), 56–57, 61 (first

The first excerpt on page 92 is from *A Few of the Sayings, Instructions, and Prayers of the Foundress of the Sisters of Mercy* (New York: The Catholic Publication Society, 1877), page 52.

The second excerpt on page 99 is from "Editor's Introduction," by John S. Mogabgab, in *Weavings*, vol. 9, November–December 1994, pages 2–3.

The excerpts on pages 109 (first excerpt), 109 (second excerpt), 109 (third excerpt), 109 (fourth excerpt), and 110 (first excerpt) are from *Cottage Controversy*, by Mother M. Catherine McAuley, edited by Mother Mary Teresa Austin Carroll (Baltimore: Lowry and Lubman Printers, 1964), pages 3, 7, 5, 32–33, and 29, respectively. Used with permission of the Sisters of Mercy, Dublin, Ireland.

The fourth excerpt on page 110 is from *Thoughts from the Spiritual Conferences of Mother M. Catherine McAuley*, by the Sisters of Mercy (Dublin, Ireland: M. H. Gill and Son, n.d.), pages 17–18.

The excerpt on page 117 is from "Spirit: Resource for Healing," by Rachel Naomi Remen, in *Noetic Sciences Review*, number 27, Autumn 1993, page 62.

Titles in the Companions for the Journey Series

Praying with Anthony of Padua	forthcoming
Praying with Benedict	forthcoming
Praying with Catherine McAuley	
Praying with Catherine of Siena	
Praying with Clare of Assisi	
Praying with Dominic	
Praying with Dorothy Day	
Praying with Elizabeth Seton	
Praying with Francis of Assisi	
Praying with Hildegard of Bingen	
Praying with Ignatius of Loyola	
Praying with John Baptist de La Salle	
Praying with John of the Cross	
Praying with Julian of Norwich	
Praying with Louise de Marillac	
Praying with Teresa of Ávila	
Praying with Thérèse of Lisieux	
Praying with Thomas Merton	
Praying with Vincent de Paul	

Order from your local religious bookstore or from

Saint Mary's Press
702 TERRACE HEIGHTS
WINONA MN 55987-1320
USA
1-800-533-8095